COMIC BOOKS

ORIGIN STORIES

Publications International, Ltd.

Contributing writer: Ron Goulart

Cover art: Animirth Comics, Inc.; Centaur Publications, Inc.; Comic Magazine Corp.; Creston Publications Corp.; DC Comics, Inc.; Dell Publishing Co.; Educational Comics, Inc.; Fables Publishing Co., Inc.; Famous Funnies, Inc.; Fawcett Publications, Inc.; Fox Publications, Inc.; Magazine Enterprises, Inc.; M.L.J. Magazines, Inc.; Newsstand Publications, Inc.; Oskar Lebeck; R.S. Callender; Street & Smith Publications, Inc.; United Feature Syndicate, Inc.; Vital Publications, Inc.

Interior backgrounds and decorations: Shutterstock.com

Louis Weber, CEO
Publications International, Ltd.
8140 Lehigh Avenue
Morton Grove, IL 60053

Permission is never granted for commercial purposes.

ISBN: 978-1-68022-508-2

Manufactured in China.

8 7 6 5 4 3 2 1

CONTENTS

INTRODUCTION: AN ENDURING AMERICAN ART FORM 4

CHAPTER 1: HOW IT BEGAN.. 6

CHAPTER 2: THE BANDWAGON STARTS TO ROLL 21

CHAPTER 3: "EVERYTHING IS BRAND NEW." 32

CHAPTER 4: HEROES FOR SALE 48

CHAPTER 5: "IT'S . . . SUPERMAN!"................................. 58

CHAPTER 6: THE BOOM YEARS.. 78

CHAPTER 7: LAFF IT UP!.. 106

CHAPTER 8: GIRLS! ROMANCE! HORRORS!......................... 123

INTRODUCTION
An Enduring American Art Form

The diversity of comic books over the 50-plus years of their history has been remarkable. Readers have enjoyed coy, pin-up girl tease...

©1964 by Super

...and rousing science fiction adventure.

©1957 by National Periodical Publications, Inc.

As the twentieth century became the twenty-first, the comic book industry had seen more than its share of ups and downs. According to some estimates, annual sales had peaked at $1 billion during the 1990s, though they had backed off from that by the year 2000. The average comic book cost just around three dollars, with 300 to 400 new issues released from more than three dozen different publishers each month. In 1934, the first year that modern-format comic books were available on newsstands, selling at ten cents a copy, a reader could have purchased the industry's entire annual output for less than one dollar. In the course of the colorfully illustrated history that follows, we'll trace the growth of the comic book industry from that humble start in the 1930s to the boom years of the 1940s and early 1950s.

The comic book format that was developed in the thirties still prevails today. To millions of readers over the years, the colorful pamphlet with slick covers and a pulp-paper interior has been a convenient and inexpensive form of entertainment. For more than 80 years, then, the comic book has remained a popular and appealing storytelling medium.

This book's coverage includes the leading types of comics that have excited readers of all ages over the 80 years. Superheroes, cowboys, spacemen, teenagers, jungle women, gangsters, young lovers, monsters—all of these and many more have played out their adventures in comic books' four-color pages, and all began and thrived in the first two decades.

Starting with the books and magazines that were the antecedents of comic books in the early years of this century, we'll trace the development of the medium from its first great surge of popularity in the Depression years through the boom-time "Golden Age" of the 1940s. Throughout the book, illuminating sidebars discuss notable comic book artists, writers, and publishers; popular characters; and unusual types of comic books.

Along the way, hundreds of full-color covers (including many rare collectors' items), interior pages, and individual panels help tell the story of the vibrant, uniquely American art form known to countless millions of fans as the comic book. These classic books built the foundation for the superhero revival beginning in the 1970s and for the unbelievable explosion of 21st century movies and television shows set in these heroes' universes.

The enduring appeal of comic books first catalyzed in the 1930s, when publishers adapted to demand and created original characters. The industry continues to adapt, grow, and mutate to suit each new generation of readers. Join us as we look at where it all began.

Comic book fans have been whisked away to remarkable adventures on other worlds, thrilled to the exploits of superheroes such as the Sandman . . .

. . . met pretty girls under the sea, and seen colorful jungle action. It's a mixture of fantasy and fun that readers find irresistible.

CHAPTER 1

How It Began

Famous Funnies was the first of the modern-format comic books, and its success sparked what became a multi-million-dollar industry. This 1941 cover with Fearless Flint is by H. G. Peter, the first artist to draw Wonder Woman.

©1941 by Famous Funnies, Inc.

*T*he story of comic books really begins with newspaper comics. Long a popular part of America's newspapers, comic strips amused readers with simple, often farcical humor and drawings. By the tail end of the 19th century, newspaper funnies were going strong--at least on Sundays. Comic books of various sizes and shapes, all of them reprinting newspaper strips, showed up soon thereafter. The first decade of the 20th century saw an assortment of comic books; among the earliest titles were *The Yellow Kid*, *The Katzenjammer Kids*, and *Buster Brown*. Comics featuring these characters were successful, but the character most frequently seen in comic books during the years between the turn of the century and the advent of World War I was Carl Schultze's Foxy Grandpa. From 1901 to 1916 more than two dozen books reprinted "Bunny" Schultze's rather inane page about a clever old coot who was forever outfoxing his two prankish nephews. The feature began in 1900 in the New York *Herald*, a newspaper that had a hand in the earliest reprint publications.

The books, some of which were hardcovers, were colorful and ranged from twenty-four to fifty-two pages. They measured as large as 10 inches by 15 inches and as small as 6½ by 7¾.

Nearly as successful as Foxy Grandpa in these first fifteen years of the new century was Buster Brown. A creation of Richard

F. Outcault, he was a sort of devilish Katzenjammer Kid inhabiting the body and outfit of a sissified Little Lord Fauntleroy. Between 1903 and 1917 Buster appeared in nearly two dozen reprint comic books of various shapes, sizes, and colors. Winsor McCay's *Little Nemo*, now considered the best strip to come out of these early years, made it into only two comic books during the same period. One was an 11 by 16½-inch color reprint of Sunday pages issued in 1906 and another, measuring 10 by 14, in 1909. McCay's dreamlike masterpiece was not reprinted again until 1945.

As noted above, the newspapers themselves were among the earliest publishers of comic books. Late in 1902 William Randolph Hearst's New York Journal introduced five titles, described as being "the best comic-books that have ever been published." Each book had cardboard covers, reprinted Sunday pages in color, and sold for 50 cents. The titles, available from Hearst newspaper dealers across the country, included Rudolph Dirks's *The Katzenjammer Kids* and F.B. Opper's *Happy Hooligan*. A book of Jimmy Swinnerton's kid strip *Jimmy* was released in 1905. That same year the *Herald* reprinted Winsor McCay's *Little Sammy Sneeze*.

Much of the color went out of comic books in the second decade of the

century, when the black and white format became the industry standard. The daily comic strip, with Bud Fisher's pioneering *Mutt & Jeff* as the role model, was becoming increasingly popular. Fisher's strip made its debut in 1907 and enjoyed considerable popularity into the 1940s. By about 1920, just about every newspaper in America would be running a full page of black and white strips six days a week. Ball Publications, in collaboration with Fisher, published its initial *Mutt and Jeff Cartoons* book in 1910. Selling for 50 cents, the book measured approximately 5 by 15 inches and reprinted only one daily strip on each page. In his kidding preface Fisher, one of the first cartoonists to benefit greatly from character merchandising, admitted that the only excuse for publishing the book was "to get the money." Get it he did, since sales figures on the first book prompted Ball to publish four more over the next six years.

The lanky, chinless Mutt—mean-minded and henpecked—had begun his strip life as a compulsive race track addict. Mutt's companion, the diminutive and dapper Jeff, always played the wise fool. Their funny-paper escapades were like daily doses of vaudeville comedy.

The largest and most successful publisher of comic books during the first three decades of the century was a now forgotten company, Cupples & Leon. Based in Manhattan, the firm published

The newspaper-strip adventures of Rudolph Dirks's incorrigibly bratty Katzenjammer Kids were among the earliest to be reprinted in "comic book" form.

©Rudolph Dirks

more than one hundred different issues of a variety of comic book titles between 1906 and 1934. The company issued the majority of its output in the 1920s. Like almost all of its competitors in the then uncrowded comic book field, Cupples & Leon reprinted newspaper comics, and offered no original material. Among the earliest Cupples & Leon titles were *Buster Brown* and *Little Nemo*.

Victor Cupples and Arthur Leon founded their company in 1902. "The idea that enabled it to establish itself as a publishing house," as historian John Tebbel has pointed out, "was the partners' discovery that there was a market for bound collections of comic strips." In 1916 Cupples & Leon introduced a line of black and white comic books when they assumed the reprinting of *Mutt & Jeff*. These forty-eight-page books were 9½ inches square and had flexible cardboard covers printed in black and red. Each page

offered a single daily strip, cut in half and run in two tiers. The price was 25 cents.

C & L added reprints of Sidney Smith's *The Gumps* in 1918 and George McManus's *Bringing Up Father* in 1919. This series of two-bit books proved extremely popular with readers. The American News Co. sold them on newsstands and also aboard railroad trains, a popular market during the period. According to Tebbel, "One of the largest contracts ever negotiated in publishing up to that time was the contract Cupples & Leon signed in 1921, when American News bought $405,000 worth of these comic books."

The most popular Cupples & Leon title was *Bringing Up Father*, which appeared in twenty-six different 25-cent issues and two 75-cent Big Book editions. Next in popularity was *Mutt & Jeff*, with sixteen paperbacks and three hardcovers. Also popular were reprint

collections of *Little Orphan Annie*, *The Gumps*, and *Tillie the Toiler*. The *Annie* books, reprinting the melodramatic adventures of Harold Gray's reactionary, redheaded moppet, were ninety-two-page hardcovers with dust jackets. The books measured 7¼ by 8½ inches and sold for 60 cents each. Other strips packaged

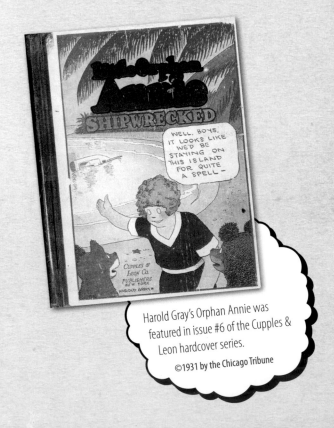

Harold Gray's Orphan Annie was featured in issue #6 of the Cupples & Leon hardcover series.

this way included *Smitty* and *Reg'lar Fellers*.

Toward the end of the company's involvement with the funnies C & L reprinted three of the strips that would become staples of the modern-format, full color comic books during the 1930s—*Joe Palooka*, *Tailspin Tommy*, and *Dick Tracy*. In 1934, after publishing final issues of *Little Orphan Annie* and *Bringing Up Father*, Cupples & Leon bid farewell to comics. It's ironic to note that the company's address at the time was 470 Fourth Avenue in New York City, not far from where another key player in comic book history, Major Malcolm Wheeler- Nicholson, would eventually set up shop.

In addition to comic books, Cupples & Leon pioneered the publishing of children's fiction in inexpensive hardcover formats. The company began a relationship with the enterprising Edward Stratemeyer in 1906 to launch a line of 50-cent novels. Stratemeyer, a writer and entrepreneur, was what would today be called a packager. He created characters and formats, then farmed the actual writing out to others. He had a hand in the creation of the Rover Boys, Tom Swift, and a pair of series that are still going strong today: Nancy Drew and the Hardy Boys. Of more than thirty major children's-book series published by Cupples & Leon before World War II, at least fifteen were turned out by

Stratemeyer and his crew. A married couple, Howard and Lilian Garis, took care of many of the rest.

The Stratemeyer Syndicate's first series for C & L featured the Motor Boys—*The Motor Boys in Mexico*, *The Motor Boys Afloat*, et al—and credited the series to Clarence Young, a pen name. Stratemeyer produced many other series for C & L, including books about Baseball Joe, Dave Dashaway, the Boy Hunters, the Radio Girls, the Four Little Blossoms, and Bomba the Jungle Boy. Early on, Cupples & Leon touted the Motor Boys as "the biggest and best selling series for boys ever published." Eventually, the firm was selling more than a million copies of its various fiction titles each year.

Other publishers flirted with comic books from 1910 to 1930. The Saalfield Company, successful with low-priced kids' books since 1900, issued several titles in 1917. Among them were *Hawkshaw the Detective* and Rudolph Dirks's *Hans und Fritz*. Measuring roughly 10 by 13, the books contained thirty-two pages of black and white Sunday-strip reprints, four panels to a page. Charlie Chaplin became a comic book character in 1917, when the M. A. Donohue Company of Chicago started a series of large black and white books reprinting the *Charlie Chaplin's Comic Capers* newspaper strip drawn by E. C. Segar. Clare Briggs's *Ain't It A Grand*

and Glorious Feeling? was reprinted in 1922 and Harry Tuthill's *Home, Sweet Home* (which later became *The Bungle Family*) appeared in 1925.

Edgar Rice Burroughs's famous jungle man made both his comic strip and his comic book debut in 1929. The daily

A typical day with the Bungles, from their 1925 comic book.

©1925 by the M.C. Donahue Co.

Hawkshaw the Detective: An early comic book reprinting Gus Mager's Holmesian spoof.

©1917 by Saalfield Publishing Co.

strip adaptation of *Tarzan of the Apes*, drawn by Hal Foster, started in January. Later that year Grosset & Dunlap issued *The Illustrated Tarzan Book*, which reprinted the first seventy-eight strips. Although the cover of the 50-cent book said No. 1, there never was a second one. When the book was reissued in the Depression year of 1934, the price was cut to 25 cents.

Mickey Mouse, cinema star since the late 1920s, first appeared in comic books in 1931. These, published by the

David McKay Co. of Philadelphia, reprinted the *Mickey Mouse* newspaper strips that were drawn by Floyd Gottfredson. The books appeared annually through 1934; three of them offered dailies in black and white and the other reprinted Sunday strips in color.

A pair of books that reprinted E. C. Segar's *Thimble Theatre* strip were published by the Sonnet Publishing Co. of Manhattan in 1931 and 1932. The books were priced at 25 cents each and appeared in a format similar to the one

established by Cupples & Leon. In 1935 David McKay published two reprint books of Segar's strip, naming them after its star, Popeye. That same year McKay issued a comic book reprinting Carl Anderson's pantomime strip *Henry*. Both these strips were syndicated by Hearst's King Features. As we'll see, when King went into the full color, modern-format comic book business in 1936, it was in partnership with McKay.

In a sense, the type of comic books we've been considering thus far are still with us. Books that reprint a newspaper strip in either paperback or hardcover format have continued to thrive to this day. The best-selling trade paperback collections of *Peanuts*, *Garfield*, and *Calvin and Hobbes* are obvious examples.

About the only thing that came close to resembling a contemporary comic book in the years from 1900 to 1930 was an experimental magazine called *Comic Monthly*. It first hit the newsstands in January 1922, with each issue devoted to a different comic strip. The magazine sold for a dime, gave the reader twenty-four pages with a black and white daily on each page, and measured 8½ by 10 inches. It had a soft paper cover printed in red and black and was published by the Embee Distributing Co. of New York City. As comics historian Charles Wooley has pointed out, the format owed a great deal to that of Cupples & Leon's line of 25- cent

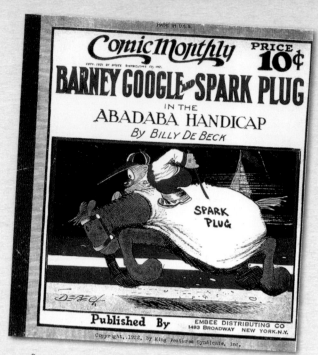

Barney Google heads for the wire on the cover of the eleventh issue of *Comic Monthly*, the first regularly issued comic book.

©1922 by King Features Syndicate, Inc.

Classic "bigfoot" cartoon style, as exemplified by Gordon "Boody" Rogers's *Deadwood Gulch*.

©1931 by Dell Publishing

comic books. But because of the 10-cent price, the cheaper paper and, most importantly, that it appeared on a regular monthly schedule, *Comic Monthly* was much closer to the comic books that would emerge in the 1930s.

The first title in the twelve-issue *Comic Monthly* series was Cliff Sterrett's *Polly & Her Pals*. Next came Rube Goldberg's *Mike & Ike*, followed by C. M. Payne's *S'Matter, Pop?* Subsequent reprints included *Barney Google*, *Tillie the Toiler*, *Little Jimmy*, and *Toots & Casper*.

As mentioned above, the Embee Distributing Co. was involved in early comic book publishing. The *Em* in the company name stood for cartoonist George McManus, creator of *Bringing Up Father*. His strip had been one of Cupples & Leon's best-selling titles since 1919, which probably accounts for the similarity in appearance between the two lines. The *bee* in Embee was Ruldolph Block, Jr. His father had joined the Hearst organization in 1896 and became comics editor of the *Journal and American*. A man not much admired by most of the cartoonists who had to work with him, Block, Sr. had been involved with the development of many of the major Hearst comic strips from *The Katzenjammer Kids* onward. Block, Jr. served as editor of *Comic Monthly*, not surprisingly, most of the strips reprinted in the magazine were from the Hearst

syndicates. Obviously ahead of its time, the magazine survived for just one year before folding.

Early in 1929 George Delacorte, founder of the Dell Publishing Company, also tried his hand at inventing the modern comic book. What he actually produced, though, looked more like a tabloid funny paper section. Delacorte had concluded that the best part of the Sunday newspaper was the comic section and set out to produce one of his own. *The Funnies* was a twenty-four-page tabloid with a third of its pages in color. It came out each week and sold for 10 cents. In its pages could be found such original features as *Frosty Ayre* by Joe Archibald, *My Big Brudder* by Tack Knight, *Deadwood Gulch* by Boody Rogers, and *Clancy the Cop* by Vic E. Pazmino (VEP).

The Funnies struggled along for thirty-six issues before expiring. The editor of the brave but doomed venture was Harry Steeger, who went on to become a major publisher of pulp fiction magazines in the 1930s and 1940s—*The Spider*, *Dime Detective*, and others—and never had anything to do with another comic book. Dell briefly tried the black and white format as well, adopting the Cupples & Leon style. In 1930 they issued VEP's *Clancy the Cop*. The following year came Rogers's *Deadwood Gulch*, plus a second *Clancy*. Although drawn in comic strip form, the material was original.

Just before the publication of the earliest modern-style comic books, a particularly novel method of recycling newspaper comic strips appeared when the Whitman Publishing Company of Racine, Wisconsin, introduced its first Big Little Book (BLB) in 1932. Sold mainly in 5-and-10- cent stores, these plump, board-covered books usually measured 3½ by 4½ inches and contained between three hundred and four hundred pages. They were miniature, illustrated novels in which each page of text was followed by a drawing. The text was based on the narrative of the comic strip sequence being adapted; the pictures were actual panels from the strip. Unfortunately, the artwork had to be butchered—dialogue balloons were whited out and the drawings were tinkered with to make them fit the standard BLB page size.

The Adventures of Dick Tracy was the very first BLB title, followed in 1933 by *Buck Rogers*, *25th Century A.D.*; *Little Orphan Annie*; *Chester Gump at Silver Creek Ranch*; *Tarzan of the Apes*; and *Reg'lar Fellers*. Whitman also introduced a few originals, including one about cowboys and adaptations of *Robinson Crusoe* and *Treasure Island*.

Big Little Books continued to be published throughout the thirties and forties, although the name was changed to Better Little Books in 1938. Nearly three hundred different titles were issued during the first five years. Although these 10-cent BLBs used many of the same characters that were starting to appear in comic books—*Dick Tracy*, *Mickey Mouse*, *Tarzan*, *the Lone Ranger*, *Buck Rogers*, *Wash Tubbs*, *Gene Autry*, *Little Orphan Annie*, *Flash Gordon*— they were able to co-exist peacefully with their four-color competition. This was chiefly because Big Little Books and the several knockoff imitators that sprang up— including Saalfield's Little Big Book line— sold exclusively in the five-and-dime market, in chain and variety stores. The new comic books, on the other hand, were sold chiefly through newsstands.

According to John Tebbel, the average initial print run for a BLB title was between 250,000 and 350,000 copies. Lawrence Lowery, a leading authority on the genre, says authors of the original-material titles were "generally paid a $250 advance on royalties to write a manuscript. The royalties were one-quarter cent per book, and the amount was usually split between the author and the artist." The average hardcover mystery novel in the 1930s, by the way, didn't pay a much larger advance.

To illustrate its original titles, Whitman built up an interesting stable of artists that included Fred Harman, Henry E. Vallely, Ken Ernst, Bud Sagendorf, and Erwin L. Hess.

They Raced Across the Lawn

This suspenseful scene from Junior G-Men is a typical Big Little Book illustration.

Whitman also experimented with black and white hardcover reprint books in 1934, publishing four issues of a *Famous Comics* series. These contained sixty-four pages and measured 7 by 8 inches. Included among the reprinted strips were Dirks's *The Captain and the Kids* and Merrill Blosser's *Freckles and his Friends*. As late as 1941, long after Whitman had gone into the four-color comic book business, the company introduced a Better Little Book series called *All Picture Comics*. These titles, which printed one unaltered strip panel per page, included *Dan Dunn*, *Smitty*, and *Smokey Stover*.

The first regularly published comic book in the standard format was *Famous Funnies*. Remember that title; although *Famous Funnies* got off to a shaky start and didn't climb out of the red until it had been in business for more than six months, it became the cornerstone of what was to become one of the most lucrative branches of magazine publishing. Not only was *Famous Funnies* the first comic book in the modern format, it was also the first, with the exception of *The Funnies*, to feature more than one character. For anyone who had a dime in the Depression year of 1934, *Famous Funnies* offered dozens of characters, all of them from the newspapers. The lineup included *Joe Palooka*, *Dixie Dugan*, *Connie*, *Hairbreadth Harry* and the perennially popular *Mutt & Jeff*. *Buck Rogers* was added in the third issue. The covers promised "100 comics and games," which was good enough to eventually attract legions of faithful readers.

The creator of *Famous Funnies* — which is essentially the comic book as we know it today—appears to be a man named Harry I. Wildenberg. The reason there's no shock of recognition when you hear Wildenberg's name is because he came up with his innovative

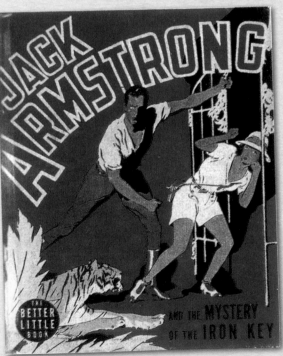

A selection of Big Little Books and Better Little Books. Kids loved the books' handy size, action-packed narratives, and exciting illustrations.

idea while working for someone else. He worked for the Eastern Color Printing Company of Waterbury, Connecticut, as sales manager. One of the things Eastern Color did was print the Sunday comic sections of several East Coast newspapers. Having an advertising background, Wildenberg first thought of using the comics as advertising premiums. He sold Gulf Oil the idea of giving away a tabloid-size book of comics at its gas stations. The gimmick was a successful one, and Wildenberg continued to refine the idea. While contemplating extensions of *the funnies* as a premium, Wildenberg and some of his associates noticed that reduced Sunday pages they had made as a promotion for the Philadelphia *Ledger* would fit two to a page on a standard tabloid-size sheet of paper. Further fiddling and figuring enabled Wildenberg to work out a way to use Eastern's presses to print sixty-four-page, color comic books.

The next problem was what to do with the resultant magazines. Wildenberg, with the help of an Eastern salesman named M. C. Gaines, first interested other advertisers in using comic books as premiums. Eastern produced books for Procter & Gamble, Canada Dry, Kinney Shoes, Wheatena, and other manufacturers of kid-oriented products. These giveaway editions usually had print runs ranging from 100,000 to 250,000,

but some went as high as one million copies.

Wildenberg and Gaines then considered sticking a 10-cent price tag on their comic books and selling them directly to children. With this, one of the great ideas of publishing history had been hatched. The pair approached the Woolworth's chain as a possible outlet but were told that sixty-four pages of old comics didn't offer sufficient value for a dime. Eventually, in 1934, Wildenberg persuaded the American News Company to distribute a monthly comic book to newsstands across the country. He called the new magazine *Famous Funnies*, a title he'd originally thought of for a soap company premium. The initial issue sold ninety percent of its 200,000 copies. Although Eastern Color lost over $4,000 on that one, by issue #12 *Famous* was netting $30,000 a month. Wildenberg admitted, in a profile of him that appeared years later in *The Commonweal*, that he never read the funnies himself. He "didn't understand how anyone else could, but he could see [the funnies'] commercial possibilities."

Editorial offices for the fledgling magazine were set up in Manhattan. Although Harold A. Moore, a longtime Eastern Color employee, was listed as editor, the actual working editor of *Famous Funnies* was Stephen A. Douglas. Brooklyn born, Douglas was working as a professional cartoonist

before he even reached his teens. He was in his late twenties when he went to work as an editor and production manager for *Famous*. Among Douglas's responsibilities was to take the syndicate proofs of the strips and get them ready to be printed. This involved, unfortunately, relettering, enlarging, and sometimes cutting the copy in the balloons and captions so that the whole ▶

A typical sampling from the *Hairsbreadth Harry* series in *Famous Funnies*. The first comic book in the modern format, Famous Funnies got off to a shaky start, but eventually revolutionized the publishing industry.

M.C. Gaines

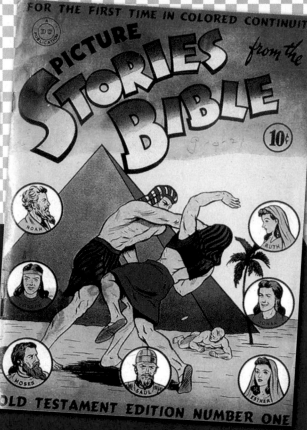

M. C. Gaines was a publishing veteran with an astute sense of what youngers wanted to read. *Picture Stories from the Bible* was just one of Gaines's many successes.

©1942 by M. C. Gaines

His full name was Maxwell Charles Gaines, but most people called him Charlie. A natural entrepreneur, Gaines was an important figure in the development of modern comic books. He played a part in launching *Famous Funnies*, packaged such early reprint titles as *Popular Comics* , helped discover Superman, and published the comic books that introduced heroic characters like Hawkman, the Flash, the Atom, the Green Lantern, and Wonder Woman.

Born in 1896, Gaines first worked as a salesman. While employed by Eastern Color, he teamed with Harry Wildenberg to get *Famous Funnies* going and onto the newsstands. In the middle 1930s, while working at the McClure Syndicate, he used McClure's color presses to print a line of comic books for Dell. Aided by youthful cartoonist/editor Sheldon Mayer, Gaines put together *Popular Comics*, *The Funnies*, and *The Comics*. At Mayer's suggestion, he advised DC to print Superman. Finally, late in 1938, Gaines entered into partnership with DC to produce comic books. His titles eventually included *All-American Comics*, *Flash Comics*, *All Star Comics*, and *Sensation Comics*.

Despite his association with some of the most successful superheroes of the Golden Age, Gaines never was especially fond of that type of character. He believed comic books could be used for educational purposes. While still with DC, he persuaded the company to   *Picture Stories From The Bible*. The seven issues of this series, begun in 1942, eventually sold several million copies. Gaines donated part of his profits from the enterprise to religious groups, telling them he considered the Bible comic books not a business venture but rather "a public service."

Gaines parted with DC in 1945 to found Educational Comics, Inc. By concentrating on comic books devoted to history and science, EC racked up some impressive sales. Unfortunately, the first part of the EC story came to an end in the summer of 1947, when M.C. Gaines was killed in a boating accident. The company was inherited by his son, William, who went on to make some comic book history of his own.

package wouldn't reproduce too small. Minuscule lettering became a source of criticism for the early reprint comic books, where Sunday pages usually ran at one-fourth of their intended newspaper size. The first original-material magazines that came along a year or so after the debut of *Famous Funnies* stressed the fact that their comics were ones "you can read without hurting your eyes." Douglas also had to extend a panel here and there to make it fit the pages just right, and he would white out any dot patterns that might interfere with the laying on of color.

During its early days, *Famous Funnies* reprinted mostly Sunday pages. Among the few exceptions were a sports strip called *Ned Brant* and an aviation strip, *Flying to Fame*. Besides those mentioned earlier, some of the other Sunday pages reprinted were *Tailspin Tommy*, *The Bungle Family*, *Jane Arden* (complete with paper dolls), *Toonerville Folks*, and *The Nebbs*. Except for the two-page text story at the center of each issue, there was no original material to be found in the first few issues.

Gradually some original filler pages started to show up, though none were drawn by Douglas, who didn't have a chance to use his own work in the magazine for several years. The earliest contributor was Victor E. Pazmino. A man with an affinity for being present at the creation of significant things, VEP

had been a contributor to *The Funnies* in 1929. For *Famous Funnies* he drew a monthly page of gag cartoons as well as a page about Seaweed Sam, a bubble-nosed, hard-traveling sailor who was fond of speaking in verse. Nearly all the covers during the magazine's first seven years were drawn by VEP He had an appealingly loose, simple style, one that looked as though it had probably stopped developing when he was about ten years old. Other early fillers were supplied by Bob Bliss, who contributed a page about a little girl named Queenie, and M. E. Brady, who brought two cartoon lads named Buttons and Fatty over from the Brooklyn Eagle and rechristened them Butty and Fatty.

As it moved into its third year, *Famous Funnies* made considerable changes in its contents. Several of the top Associated Press-syndicate strips, including *Scorchy Smith*, *Dickie Dare*, *Oaky Doaks*, and *The Adventures of Patsy*, were added. That meant the magazine was now offering artwork by some of the most gifted newspaper artists of the 1930s—men such as Noel Sickles, Milton Caniff, Ralph B. Fuller, Mel Graff, Coulton Waugh, and Bert Christman. Late in 1937, when the Register & Tribune Syndicate and the McNaught Syndicate decided to go into the comic book business on their own (the result was Feature Funnies), *Famous Funnies* lost *Joe Palooka*, *Dixie*

Dugan, *Jane Arden*, and several other popular features. By the end of the decade, *Famous Funnies* had a lineup that included—in addition to the Associated Press strips and *Buck Rogers*—*Roy Powers, Eagle Scout* by

Seaweed Sam, the Rhyming Rover, sails with his pal Tiny into a potentially dangerous situation.

©1941 by Famous Funnies, Inc.

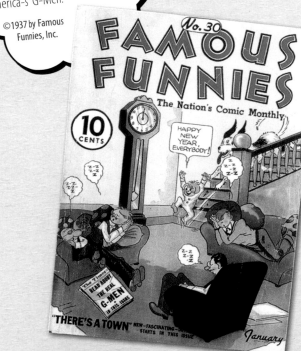

Frank Godwin, *Skyroads* by Russell Keaton, and *Big Chief Wahoo* by Allen Saunders and Elmer Woggon.

In issue #62 (September 1939) two pages of *Lightnin' and the Lone Rider* dailies were added to each issue. This cowboy strip, which differed from *The Lone Ranger* only in that its hero didn't ride a white horse or have an Indian companion, was drawn by a young fellow who used the snappy pen name of Lance Kirby. As "Jack" Kirby he'd produce work of much greater originality, and win countless fans over a span of five decades.

Famous Funnies also reprinted Lone Rider strips by Kirby's successor, Frank Robbins. *Speed Spaulding* was eventually added to the magazine's lineup, in four-page chunks. This was science fiction based on the Edwin Balmer-Philip Wylie novel *When Worlds Collide*; the feature was illustrated by Marvin Bradley, who later graduated to *Rex Morgan, MD.*, a long-running newspaper strip. Another fantasy strip, Russell Stamm's *Invisible Scarlet O'Neil*, bowed in *Famous Funnies* #81 (April 1941).

By this time the superhero deluge had hit comic books and *Famous Funnies* was starting to worry about the competition. The magazine's sales figures climbed to a peak of over 400,000 copies a month in 1939, but by 1941 had skidded to

Dick Calkins's *Buck Rogers* is one of the classic science fiction newspaper strips. It was a popular feature of *Famous Funnies*.

©1941 by Famous Funnies, Inc.

just a little over 250,000. Until then the covers had been whimsical, showing various characters in gag situations. But the cover on issue #81 was a dramatic one, depicting Scarlet O'Neil rescuing a child from a fire. Artwork was by H. G. Peter, who would go over to DC in 1942 to draw *Wonder Woman*.

This new approach would be the start of a trend and the next nine *Famous Funnies* covers were all serious and showed the likes of *Buck Rogers*, *Scorchy Smith*, and *Dickie Dare* in action situations. Two of these actionful covers

Oaky Doaks was appealing drawn by Ralph B. Fuller and also drew audiences for *Famous Funnies*.

Famous Funnies won fans with M. E. Brady's innocuously amusing kid strip *Butty and Fatty*.

Elmer Woggon's *Big Chief Wahoo*, popular in *Famous Funnies*, began as a gag strip but morphed into a realistic adventure strip much later.

were by Bill Everett, creator of Sub-Mariner.

Going even further in trying to hold its own against Superman, Batman, and the hordes of other costumed heroes who were taking over the newsstands, *Famous Funnies* came up with a superhero of its own for issue #89, dated December, 1941. Created by Douglas and drawn by Peter, the character was named Fearless Flint, a fellow who started life as an ordinary guy named Jack Bradley. Bradley had one of the more proletarian backgrounds

among the heroes and was not the usual bored playboy or mild mannered reporter. When first encountered, he was operating a jackhammer on the Mt. Rushmore sculptures. An explosion transformed him into "A MAN FROM FLINT . . . with the strength of 10 men." Flint's costume consisted of a pair of white riding pants and boots. He went around bare-chested, the better to show off the fact that his skin turned a bright crimson when he went into his heroic phase. If this sounds dubious to you, don't worry—it didn't go over any better

with readers in the early forties. Creating topnotch heroes just wasn't Douglas's forte; Flint was extinguished after *Famous Funnies* #109.

For most of the remainder of its days *Famous Funnies* concentrated on comic strip reprints. There were fewer strips now and they were being run larger and allowed to retain their original lettering. A typical 1947 issue, for example, contained eight pages of *Steve Roper* (formerly *Big Chief Wahoo*), six pages of *Invisible Scarlet O'Neil*, six of *Dickie Dare*, six of *Scorchy Smith*, and six of *Oaky Doaks*. Four pages of *Napoleon* Sunday strips were scattered through the book. Marty Links's *Bobby Sox* panel was added in 1948, with the issue's cover admonishing readers, "Don't be an 'ICK,' be a 'FOX.' Get 'IN THE GROOVE' with BOBBY SOX." A later addition, in October of 1949, was *Ben Friday*, scripted by gag cartoonist and mystery novelist Lawrence Lariar and drawn by former Will Eisner assistant John Spranger.

An ailing bimonthly by 1950, *Famous Funnies* dropped *Buck Rogers* and replaced him with an inept science-fiction feature entitled *Barney Carr*, *Space Detective*. Barney's interplanetary career was short and he vanished after only two issues. Buck finally returned in #209 and the event was celebrated with the first of a series of eight *Buck Rogers* covers by the gifted fantasy illustrator Frank Frazetta.

The final issue of *Famous Funnies* was #218 (July 1955). It was a slim thirty-two pages, just half as thick as it had been when the title began, and contained no reprints except those of *Buck Rogers*. The rest of the issue was made up of three brand new kid features, two by Dave Gantz and one by Jack Berrill. Times had changed

but *Famous Funnies* had not changed enough to maintain its audience. Significantly, perhaps, a television set figured prominently on the final cover.

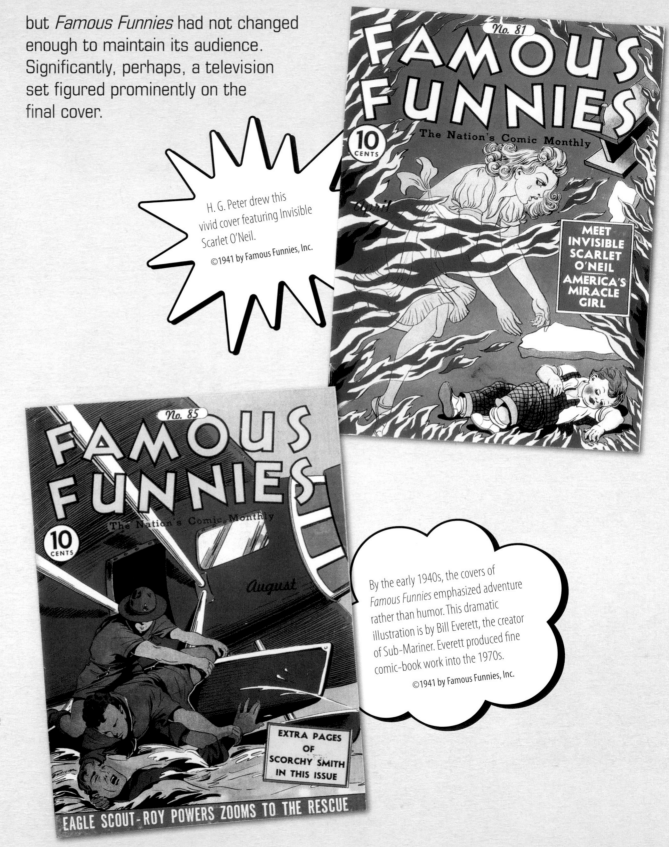

H. G. Peter drew this vivid cover featuring Invisible Scarlet O'Neil.
©1941 by Famous Funnies, Inc.

By the early 1940s, the covers of *Famous Funnies* emphasized adventure rather than humor. This dramatic illustration is by Bill Everett, the creator of Sub-Mariner. Everett produced fine comic-book work into the 1970s.
©1941 by Famous Funnies, Inc.

The most successful early modern-format comic books prospered because they offered reprints of popular newspaper strips. *The Funnies* was one of the titles that, beginning in 1935, arrived to give *Famous Funnies* some competition. The enthusiastic reception for these and other reprint comics paved the way for original characters and features and the continued growth of the comic book industry.

©1939 by Dell Publishing Co.

*T*he comic book business didn't hit high gear right away. *Famous Funnies* had the field to itself for all of its initial year and then, starting in 1935, a few other titles began to show up on newsstands. Some, inspired by *Famous*, offered reprints of popular newspaper strips. Others offered brand new material—an approach that proved to be a wise one. Readers responded so dramatically that, by 1938, the combined monthly sales of all available comic book titles were well over 2,500,000 copies. In this chapter we'll see how the fledgling industry got to that first plateau.

Late in 1935 Dell Publishing introduced *Popular Comics* (cover-dated February 1936), the first reprint title to compete with *Famous Funnies*. Although the early statements of ownership list Dell of 149 Madison Avenue, New York City, as the publisher and a gentleman named Arthur Lawson as editor, they don't tell the real story. *Popular Comics* was packaged for Dell at the offices of the McClure Syndicate, where M. C. Gaines was utilizing color presses to cash in on what he surmised would be a comic book boom. Two of the presses had been purchased from the defunct New York *Graphic*, Bernard Macfadden's impressively sleazy daily tabloid. Gaines had figured out a way to adapt the pair of two-color presses to

Popular Comics reprinted Sunday newspaper strips only. Its roster was culled from more than one syndication company. Here, chinless Andy Gump makes a resolution he won't manage to keep for long.

©1937 by Dell Publishing Co.

print four-color comic books. As noted earlier, Gaines had been in on the birth of *Famous Funnies*, and now he was involved in something nearly as significant.

Popular needed an editor and Gaines's choice was a teenage cartoonist named Sheldon Mayer. "I went to work for M. C. Gaines in January of 1936," Mayer once recalled. "I had been up to see him the previous summer, and half a year later he gave me a call and offered me a few days' pasteup work." The few days stretched into a few years and Mayer was eventually editing *Popular* as well as *The Funnies* and *The Comics*. To fill his pages, Mayer used both syndicate proofs and original strip art. The syndicates were paid about five dollars a page for reprint rights. Even though comic books were a fat sixty-four pages at that time, the pay scale didn't demand that the publisher make an enormous outlay of money.

The premiere issue of *Popular Comics* was very much in the *Famous Funnies* format, although the color was better and brighter and none of the copy had been relettered to make it larger. Only Sunday pages were reprinted. There was no original material except for the mandatory filler story at the center of the book. *Dick Tracy* led off the issue, in the midst of his tussle with the brutal Boris Arson. Strips from several rival syndicates were used, including *Skippy*, *Tailspin Tommy*, *Mutt & Jeff* (who'd also been in *Famous Funnies*), *The Gumps*, *Don Winslow*, *Little Orphan Annie*, *Bronc Peeler*, *Smokey Stover*, *Terry and the Pirates*, and *Believe It Or Not*. No attempt was made to start the reprinted sequences at the beginning of a continuity, although *Terry* did happen to commence with the first pages of the second adventure. Better-known features got four pages each month; lesser ones got two.

By the end of the first year a few changes had been made to the *Popular Comics* lineup. *Tiny Tim*, *Reg'lar Fellers*, *Smilin' Jack*, and Garret Price's handsome and imaginative *Skull Valley* had been added, and Mayer was using his own artwork to illustrate the fiction fillers. *Tom Mix* was appearing, through the courtesy of licensing-merchandising man Stephen Slesinger; the Mix adventures appear to be adaptations of Whitman Big Little Books.

By the time Mayer and Gaines ended their association with *Popular*, somewhere toward the end of 1938, the title was running fewer reprints and had added a smattering of original material. All the Chicago Tribune-New York News Syndicate pages—*Terry*, *Dick Tracy*, *Annie*, et al—had shifted over to *Super Comics* (first issue cover-dated May 1938) and been replaced by mostly original features. One such was a series of six-page adaptations of western B-movies, mostly the product of Monogram Pictures, starring such cinema cowpokes as Tex Ritter, Gene Autry, and Jack Randall. Slesinger was represented by a true-crime GMen feature drawn by his protege, Jim Gary.

Popular was now being printed by the Whitman division of Western Printing & Lithographing Company at its Poughkeepsie, New York, plant as part of a new agreement with Dell. Editorial work was done in the Manhattan office under the direction of Oskar Lebeck. A former stage designer and book illustrator, Lebeck served the magazine as artist, writer, and editor. He drew covers, wrote scripts, and initiated more new features. Among them were *The Hurricane Kids*, *The Masked Pilot*, and *Gang Busters*.

As the forties progressed the magazine gradually returned to its old reprint ways. By issue #90 (August 1943) the only original feature that remained was *Gang Busters*, which shared the pages with *Smilin' Jack*, *The Gumps*, *Toots and Casper*, and *Terry*. *Popular Comics* remained essentially a reprint comic book until the end of its days in the summer of 1948; by then it was a thin bimonthly.

The second monthly packaged for Dell by Gaines and Mayer was *The Funnies*. The first issue arrived on the stands late in the summer of 1936 (cover-dated October 1936) and was devoted to newspaper strip reprints. As mentioned in the previous chapter, Dell had already used *The Funnies* as a title for its unsuccessful original-material tabloid of 1929. Optimistic about success in a changed market, Dell resurrected the name for the new monthly. Early issues drew heavily on the stable of the Cleveland-based NEA syndicate, reprinting *Alley Oop*, *Captain Easy*, *Boots*, *Out Our Way*, *Myra North*, and *Salesman Sam*. Among the other

The Funnies was packaged for Dell Publishing by M. C. Gaines and Sheldon Mayer.
©1937 by Dell Publishing Co.

In time, The Funnies augmented its mix of whimsy and adventure reprints with original strips, creating the diverse lineup seen here.
©1940 by Dell Publishing Co.

reprints were *Dan Dunn*, *Tailspin Tommy*, *Don Dixon*, and *Bronc Peeler*. *Mutt & Jeff* was also in the lineup, suggesting that Gaines may have been superstitious about the strip; it had also been in *Famous and Popular*.

In the second issue of The Funnies editor Mayer finally got to draw a feature. It was a new one called *Scribbly*, a strip about a boy cartoonist—an appropriate character, in that Mayer himself was a "boy cartoonist." The two or three *Scribbly* pages that appeared in each issue were laid out like Sunday pages, each sporting its own logo. Mayer did this so his upstart creation could comfortably rub shoulders with the real Sunday pages being reprinted. The strip dealt with Scribbly Jibbet, who was young, small, and possessed of a head of hair resembling an untidy haystack. Mayer focused on Scribbly's efforts to break free of the bonds of home and school and into the charmed world of newspaper cartooning. Mayer has said that the strip is a blend of autobiography and fantasy, and that some of the truest-seeming elements are the most unreal. The pages mixed lower middle class apartment life with wacky excursions into the worlds of newspaper publishing, radio, and even Hollywood. It was an exuberant creation, rendered in the youthful Mayer's appealing, scribbly cartoon style.

By the end of its first year *The Funnies* had added two new, or nearly new, features. These were *G-Men on the Job* and *Og, Son of Fire*, both two-pages-per issue adaptations of already-published Big Little Books. After Gaines and Mayer ended their association with Dell, *The Funnies* underwent further changes in content and added several original strips.

The third and final magazine produced by the Gaines-Mayer team for Dell was *The Comics*. It made its debut with the March 1937 issue and, although billed originally as a monthly, took until March of 1939 to reach its eleventh issue. The Comics was a hodgepodge of reprints, reruns, and original works. The earlier issues offered reprints of *Wash Tubbs*, but the other newspaper strips that showed up in the magazine's pages were considerably less well known. From the Brooklyn Eagle's syndicate came *Bill and Davy*, a seagoing adventure done in comically exaggerated, "bigfoot" cartooning style by James McCague, and *Gordon Fife*, a strip dealing with intrigue in mythical European kingdoms. From a sparsely distributed ready-print Sunday section turned out by the George Mathew Adams Service came a cowboy strip, *Ted Strong*, by Al Carrelno; a kid adventure titled *The Enchanted Stone* by Adolphe Barreaux; and *Rod Rian of the Sky Police* by Paul Jepson. *The Comics* also reprinted *Deadwood Gulch*, *My Big*

Brudder, and *Clancy the Cop*, all of which had appeared originally in the 1929 version of *The Funnies*.

In 1936 the newspaper syndicates, which up to that time had been content to sell reprint rights to enterprising publishers, now began to take an active part in the funny book business. William Randolph Hearst's King Features Syndicate, for example, entered into an agreement with the David McKay Company to produce a comic book titled *King Comics*. United Features Syndicate, ▶

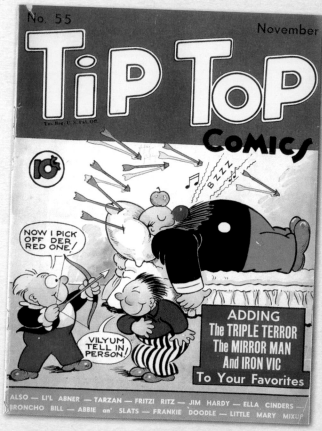

Hans and Fritz—the irrepressible Katzenjammer Kids—take aim at the snoozing Captain. *Tip Top Comics* was the first comic book published by United Feature Syndicate.

©1940 by United Feature Syndicate, Inc.

Be a Cartoonist!

Harvey Kurtzman
2166 Clinton Ave.
Bronx, New York

A runner-up i a 1939 *Tip Top* "Cartoon Club" contest was a talented young illustrator named Harvey Kurtzman— who used his unique style to create *Mad Magazine*.

©1939 by United Feature Syndicate, Inc.

One of the most interesting features in the early issues of *Tip Top Comics*, at least to the would-be cartoonists in the audience, was the section devoted to fledgling artists. It was headed with the lines—"Be a cartoonist! Join the Tip Top Cartoon Club now—it's fun!" Originally this was just a place for young cartoonists to submit their sample strips, but with issue #21 a new section was added. This involved a mustachioed western character called Buffalo Bob, who got himself into a dire predicament each month. A typical panel showed Bob falling off his ladder while painting a barn and about to land on the sharp tines of a pitchfork being held by a daydreaming farmer. "Merely draw a solution . . . find a novel way of saving poor Buffalo Bob . . . you have a chance of being a 'winner.'" As if the prospect of fame and an opportunity to save Bob's bacon weren't suffficient motivation, a one dollar prize was offered for winning solutions and original strips.

The Cartoon Club was usually given three pages each issue—a leadoff page that set up the latest Buffalo Bob dilemma, one for the winning solutions of the previous month's problem, and one for a quartet of amateur strips. The set-up page also offered news, drawing tips, and words of encouragement: "Some of the cartoons . . . are pretty close to professional standards. The improvement can be noted all down the line."

Sometimes, however, the eager young artists went too far, causing warnings to be posted. "The December BUFFALO BOB Contest taxed the imaginations of members more than usual. Entrants were asked to submit their own problems and in doing so many of them used what are know as 'editorial taboos.' We are listing them here so that other members may not make the same mistakes. 1. The use of snakes is prohibited. 2. The use of underworld characters is not allowed. 3. Solutions that point ridicule to any race, color or creed should not be used. 4. In some instances, humor due to embarrassing situations is taboo. One member sent a problem showing Buffalo Bob in shorts. It is better to steer clear of such solutions as in most cases they are unacceptable."

Because it was one of the few such outlets around (*Open Road For Boys* magazine ran a similar section), the Tip Top Cartoon Club attracted just about every aspiring cartoonist in the country. Looking back at those old pages now, one finds the names and early work of quite a few youngsters who eventually made it into professional ranks. These include Bill Yates, Jack Davis, Dan Heilman, Harvey Kurtzman, Mort Walker, and Warren Tufts. (Tufts actually managed years later to sell the strip *Casey Ruggles* to United Features, the publishers of Tip Top.) *Beetle Bailey*'s Mort Walker, when asked if he recalled sending in his work and how he felt about seeing it in print, replied that he did indeed remember. Most important to him was that he got paid, which meant he was a pro.

part of the Scripps-Howard communications empire, went *King* one better and published its own magazines. The first of these was *Tip Top Comics*, which appeared in the spring of 1936. The earliest *Tip Top* covers were drawn by Mo Leff, a United staff artist, and depicted gatherings—usually improbable —of the magazine's various characters. On the cover of the very first issue *Tarzan* and *Li'l Abner* face off in a boxing ring. *Joe Jinks* serves as referee and Mammy Yokum is her son's second. Among those gathered at ringside are *Ella Cinders*, *Fritzi Ritz*, and Hans, Fritz, and the Captain. Strange bedfellows, all! Inside these first issues were a potpourri of features, mostly reprinted Sunday pages.

Some of the pages were several years old; others, like the *Li'l Abner* Sundays, were relatively fresh. Each issue offered three *Tarzan* pages, taken from an impressive 1933 Hal Foster sequence dealing with a lost civilization patterned after ancient Egypt. Harry O'Neill's *Broncho Bill* and Leff's own boys' adventure fantasy, *Peter Pat*, provided the only serious fare. The rest of the magazine was given over to hu-

mor, supplied by the likes of *Ella Cinders*, *Fritzi Ritz*, *Looy Dot Dope*, *Joe Jinks*, *Cynical Susie*, *Danny Dingle*, *Little Mary Mixup*, *Benny*, *Billy Make Believe*, *Grin and Bear It*, and *The Captain and the Kids*. United seemed determined to get just about every strip and panel on its list packed into *Tip Top's* sixty-four pages.

Tip Top's first editor was Lev Gleason, who'd worked with Harry Wildenberg at Eastern Color. Gleason would eventually publish a number of aggressively innovative comic books, including *Boy*, *Daredevil*, and *Crime Does Not Pay*—none of which were exactly in the *Tip Top* vein. Still, by the end of its second year, *Tip Top* was leaning more toward adventure. *Tarzan* was now getting five pages and active strips like *Frankie Doodle* and Dick Moore's *Jim Hardy* had been added.

By 1945, the magazine was down to forty-eight pages and was even thinner by the late 1940s. When *Tip Top* folded in 1961, with its 225th issue, it was being published as a quarterly by Dell. The Dell issues contained brand new (and not very well done) adventures of *Nancy*, *The Captain and the Kids*, and similar fare.

United Features's second monthly, *Comics On Parade*, was launched early in 1938. The lineup was similar to what was found in *Tip Top*, except that daily versions of the strips rather than the

Sundays were reprinted. *Tarzan*, in fact, started at the very beginning of its run, with reprints of Hal Foster's handsome 1929 dailies. There were also *Fritzi Ritz*, *Li'l Abner*, and *Ella Cinders* dailies, all suitably colored for their comic book appearance, plus the rare daily *The Captain and the Kids* strips from the early 1930s. The strip was originally drawn by Rudolph Dirks and was subsequently taken over by Bernard Dibble. Wildly melodramatic plots were added, and punched up with dialogue that mixed Dirks's stage German with lines what would fit into a Marx Brothers movie. After its twenty-ninth issue (August 1940) *Comics On Parade* underwent a format change. The remaining seventy-five issues were devoted to one character per book. *Li'l Abner*, *The Captain and the Kids*, and *Nancy & Fritzi Ritz*

alternated for several years and then the frazzle-haired Nancy became the sole star until the title ceased publication in 1955. A very similar companion comic, *Sparkler Comics*, was introduced by United in the summer of 1941.

King Comics, the first McKay-Hearst title, hit the stands at the same time as *Tip Top*. Both magazines were dated April 1936 and, by chance, both used the same basic cover idea, a prizefight. On the *King* cover, Popeye wallops a gorilla while Jiggs referees. Inside, the new magazine offered a somewhat stronger lineup than its rival. On the adventure side there were Sunday pages of *Flash Gordon*, complete with *Jungle Jim* topper, *King of the Royal Mounted*, *Mandrake*, and *Tim Tyler's Luck*. Also crowded in were lesser-known adventure pages such as *Curley Harper*, *Radio Patrol*, *Little Annie Rooney*, *Ted Towers*, and *Ace Drummond*. Derring-do outweighed humor in the earliest issues of *King Comics*. Laughs were provided by Popeye in Segar's *Thimble Theatre*, *Henry*, *Bringing Up Father*, and Otto Soglow's *The Little King*. (Soglow's red-coated monarch also appeared in the magazine's logo.)

The production of *King Comics* was a joint effort that involved the Philadelphia editorial offices of the McKay Company and the King Features syndicate bullpen in Manhattan. Alexander McKay was the business manager and Ruth Plumly Thompson was the Philadelphia-based editor. Joe Musial, Bud Sagendorf, and other artists handled the

Alex Raymond was one of the greatest—and most influential—newspaper-strip artists, and his *Flash Gordon* became an American institution. Reprints of Raymond's Sunday pages were enthusiastically received by readers of *King Comics*.

The star of *Thimble Theatre* was Popeye, the rough 'n' ready swab whose popularity has continued undiminished for nearly nine decades. These newspaper strips were reprinted in *King Comics* in 1939.

New York end of things, pasting up the pages, doing covers, and so on.

Philadelphia-born Ruth Thompson is best known as the "official" successor to L. Frank Baum, writer of the *Wizard of Oz* books. Picked by Baum's publisher, Reilley & Lee, in 1921 (two years after Baum's death), Thompson turned out an Oz book a year until retiring as Royal Historian of Oz in 1939. By 1938, *King Comics's* second year, she was writing poems and text fillers for the magazine. The poems, which ran under the title *Sis Sez*, dealt with the misadventures of a freckled teenage girl and were illustrated by Marge Buell, the creator of *Little*

Lulu. Buell also drew the pictures for the Thompson fiction, which was in the Oz vein and featured such whimsical characters as King Kojo and Her Highness of Whyness.

As *King Comics* progressed, some of the marginal features were dropped and new ones were added. *Ming Foo* and *Ted Towers* left, replaced by *Barney Baxter*, *The Phantom*, and *The Lone Ranger*. Besides Miss Thompson's efforts, there was very little original material to be found in the magazine. Bob Dunn, in the days before his memorable *They'll Do It Every Time* gag panel, was in the King Features office from the middle

1930s on. When he wasn't ghosting for Milt Gross and handling other chores, he found time to provide a monthly gag page entitled *Dun-dums*. The only serious original feature to find its way into *King Comics* arrived during the magazine's second year. Laid out like a Sunday page, Jimmy Thompson's nicely done *Redmen* ran in the exact middle of the book.

Exactly a year after introducing *King Comics*, McKay introduced a title that, like *King*, was devoted to Hearst strips. Perhaps thinking of an ideal poker hand, the publisher named the new magazine *Ace Comics*. The emphasis in *Ace* was initially on the funny side. Early issues offered H. H. Knerr's expert version of the venerable *Katzenjammer Kids*, plus *Blondie*, *Tillie the Toiler*, *Barney Google*, *The Pussycat Princess*, and *Krazy Kat*. For adventure buffs, *Ace* provided heroes brought over from *King Comics*. Alex Raymond's *Jungle Jim* was the standout of a group that included *Tim Tyler*, *Curley Harer*, and Lee Falk's *The Phantom*. Hardcore students of comics will be interested to learn that McKay's own engravers were responsible for coloring the pages, which probably explains why Falk's masked mystery man wears a brown costume in comic books and a purple one in the funny papers.

Ace Comics #26 brought another actionful feature, *Prince Valiant*. In all, Ace survived until fall of 1949.

McKay's third reprint magazine came along in the summer of 1939 and was called *Magic Comics*. The star, as the title may imply, was *Mandrake the Magician*. Besides offering *Mandrake* dailies by Falk and artist Phil Davis, the early issues were used as dumping grounds for some of *King Features*'s less popular daily strips. *Inspector Wade* was to be found there, along with *Barney Baxter* and *Secret Agent X-9*. In the humor department were *Henry*, *Blondie*, and *Thimble Theatre* dailies. Jimmy Thompson drew another of his admirable features, this one called *Indian Lore*. Later issues added the dependable *Lone Ranger* and Roy Crane's *Buz Sawyer*. *Magic Comics* disappeared late in 1949, right after *Ace*. *King Comics* held on until the end of 1951.

The first issue of *Super Comics* had a cover date of May 1938 and was published by Whitman. All its reprints were from the Chicago Tribune-N.Y. News Syndicate roster. Many of the strips had already been running in *Popular* and then were switched to the new magazine, so they weren't brand new even to comic book readers who didn't have access to Trib News funnies. The stars of *Super* were *Dick Tracy* and *Terry and the Pirates*, backed up by *Smilin' Jack*, *Moon Mullins*, and *The Gumps*. In *Super's* early years most of the reprinted strips were newly colored dailies, some of them from as far back as 1935.

By the second year of *Super Comics*, Sunday pages only were being used. Since most of the continuity strips had stories that ran daily and on Sundays, this practice resulted in some perplexing gaps in the narratives. The reprints were doled out in snippets of from two to four pages per issue. Oskar Lebeck was

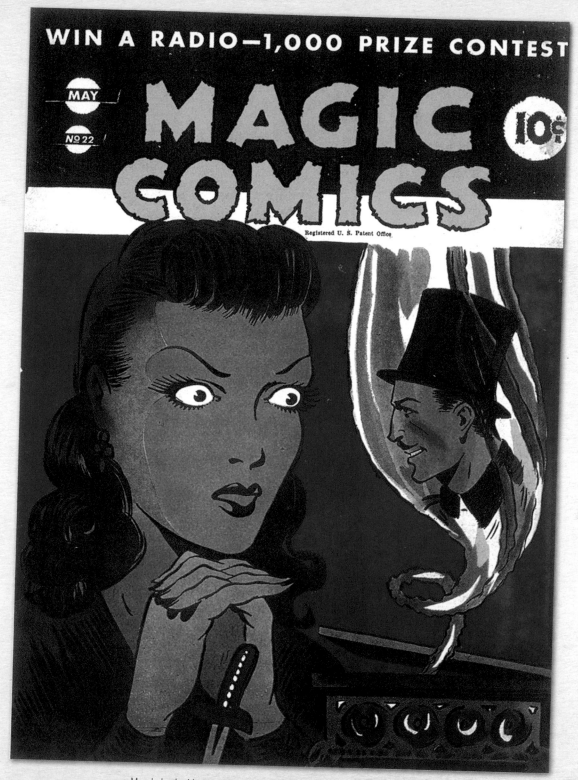

Mandrake the Magician pops in to say hello on the cover of *Magic Comics*, one of many all-reprint comic books created in the wake of *Famous Funnies*'s success.

The reprinted newspaper strips that appeared in *Super Comics* came from the Chicago Tribune-N.Y. News Syndicate. The lineup was a potent one, as this 1940 cover attests.

©1940 by R. S. Callender

Super's first editor, and also drew some of the original-material filler pages.

Toward the end of 1939, Whitman must have concluded that *Super* would have to be overhauled if it were to meet the competition from the ever-increasing number of original-material comic books. With issue #21 (February 1940), three, all-new adventure features were introduced— *Magic Morro* by Ken Ernst, *Jack Wander* by Ed Moore, and *The Thief of Bagdad* by Erwin L. Hess. The latter strip, which was based on neither of the movies of that name, was soon replaced with Richard M. Fletcher's *Jim Ellis*.

As early as the spring of 1941, Whitman apparently decided that their original characters were no match for the livelier heroes and heroines being offered by DC, Marvel, and other comic book publishers.

Whitman kept most of their characters but swung back to reprints. Beginning with issue #35 (April 1941), the tried-and- true *Dick Tracy* was featured on every cover for the next several years. By the late 1940s *Super* was again just a reprint book; the final issue, #121, was published early in 1949.

Whitman introduced *Crackajack Funnies* in the spring of 1938. The early issues had covers of uncoated, nonglossy stock, making them stand out a bit from most of the competition. Unlike some of the earlier Dell and Whitman titles, this one offered more original material mixed with reprints right from the start. The original stuff was pretty tame and revolved mainly around movie cowboys. The reprint side relied considerably on the NEA syndicate. In fact, with the exception of *Alley Oop*, the new magazine used just about the entire NEA package. *Wash Tubbs*, *Boots*, *Freckles*, *Out Our Way*, *Red Ryder*, and *Myra North* were all featured in *Crackajack's* pages. Other syndicates provided *Don Winslow*, *Dan Dunn*, and *Apple Mary*, the latter a maudlin strip that found its widest audience after changing its name to *Mary Worth*.

Saturday matinees inspired cartoon versions of western heroes Tom Mix and Buck Jones. Their adventures— rehashed BLB stories laid out in imitation Sunday-page style—had enticing titles like "The Rock Creek Cattle War" and "Kidnappers of Cholla Wash." Art was by Jim Chambers, Jim Gary, and Ken Ernst. Alden McWilliams's *Stratosphere Jim* began in *Crackerjack* #19 (January 1940), and Oskar Lebeck provided *Time Marches Back*—"The time machine is the famous invention of Looney Luke. With a simple twist of the dial it can transport him over a span of years into any age."

In *Crackajack* #23 (May 1940) the sleuth Ellery Queen made his four-color debut. The June 1940 issue introduced a costumed crimefighter, a mysterious figure of the night known as the Owl. Frank Thomas, who drew both bigfoot and straight adventure features, illustrated the Owl's nocturnal adventures beginning with the second episode.

Crackajack Funnies died with issue #43 (January 1942). Eight pages of Milton Caniff's *Terry and the Pirates* reprints were added for the last go-round and a blow-up of a Caniff panel served as the final cover. After the collapse of *Crackajack*, the Owl set up shop in *Popular Comics*, where he held on for fourteen more adventures. The success (however marginal) of this all-new character signaled the beginning of a new era in comics.

The crimfighting Owl made his debut in *Crackajack Funnies*. This moody 1941 comic is by Frank Thomas.

©1941 by K. K. Publications, Inc.

Don Winslow first appeared in newspaper strips.

©1940 by Whitman Publishing Co., Inc.

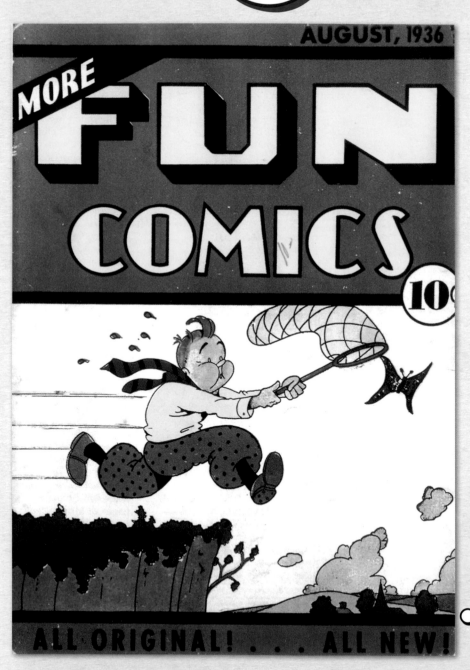

AUGUST, 1936

MORE **FUN** COMICS

10¢

ALL ORIGINAL! . . . ALL NEW!

Sometime in the autumn of 1934 Major Malcolm Wheeler-Nicholson, an erstwhile cavalry officer and pulp-magazine writer, got an idea. He made numerous notes, which he carried around Manhattan in an impressive-looking briefcase. After renting office space on Fourth Avenue, Nicholson began recruiting artists and writers and seeking financing. What he had in mind was a line of comic books that would feature nothing but original material. The company the major founded would eventually, under the name DC, earn countless millions of dollars. But Nicholson, like many a pioneer, went broke within a few years and never partook of any of these riches. They say that old soldiers just fade away, and that's what finally happened to Major Nicholson.

Initially, though, Nicholson's idea seemed full of promise. His first magazine was called *New Fun* and had a cover date of February 1935. Touted as the "big comic magazine," it was a 10- by 15-inch tabloid, taller and wider than *Famous Funnies* but nowhere near as colorful. The cover, which consisted of Lyman Anderson's *Jack Woods* cowboy page, was in full color and bordered in bright red. The thirty-two interior pages, however, were black and white. All the new strips were laid out like Sunday funnies and none, with a single exception, were given more than one page.

"All Original!" was the chief selling point of *More Fun Comics* and many new comic books that debuted beginning in 1935. No longer reliant on newspaper-strip reprints, comic books won readers with original characters and features. This *More Fun* cover was drawn by associate editor Vincent Sullivan.

©1936 by More Fun Magazine, Inc.

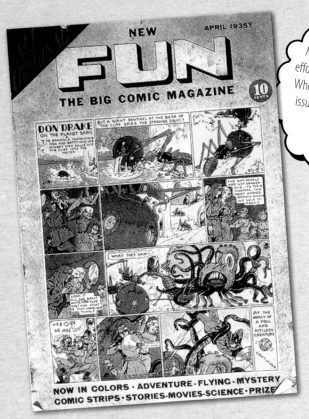

This package was an eclectic one that offered several pages of text material along with the humor and adventure strips. In addition to comics, readers got a two-page western yarn, a sports page, radio and movie news, and a popular-science page. Readers of a mechanical bent no doubt appreciated the comic's instructions for building a model plane and model boat.

The major had managed, probably through his pulp magazine (so-named for the cheap pulpwood on which they were printed) connections, to gather together quite a few ads. Not exactly aimed at kids, these included an invitation from the Gem Razor people to join the Shav-Easy Foundation, an offer from the Coyne Electrical School to divulge an "Amazingly Easy Way To Get Into Electricity," and also to send along a free booklet explaining, among other things, how to "get in on the ground floor of television." There were solicitations from two of the decade's leading mail-order musclemen, Charles Atlas and George Jowett. These advertisers, and others like them, had been longtime staples of the pulps.

Among New Fun's to-be-continued adventure features were Sandra of the Secret Service; Jack Andrews, All-American Boy (possibly a distant cousin of Jack Armstrong); Cap'n Erik; and Buckskin Jim. Lawrence Lariar contributed Barry O'Neill, a strip in the Fu Manchu tradition that pitted pipe-smoking Barry against the insidious Oriental villain Fang Gow. Lariar, a gag cartoonist and mystery novelist, later became cartoon editor of Liberty and compiler of the annual Best Cartoons albums. Henry Kiefer, a Europe-trained artist who would become one of the most prolific of comic book hacks, drew Wing Brady. This one combined two popular genres by offering a Foreign Legionnaire who was also an aviator.

Adolphe Barreaux, who drew the risque filler strip Sally the Sleuth that appeared in the Spicy Detective pulp, produced The Magic Crystal of History, a very tame, educational time-travel fantasy. Clemens Gretter took care of science fiction, drawing Don Drake of the Planet Saro and 2033/Super Police.

Because Major Nicholson didn't neglect the classics, the first issue of New Fun contained the initial installment of an adaptation of Ivanhoe. Charles Flanders, in his late twenties and a fixture in the King Features bullpen, did the drawing. He abandoned the Sir Walter Scott epic after a few issues and moved on to Treasure Island. This adaptation must originally have been intended for publication elsewhere, since the pages ended by urging readers to "see next week." The humor pages in New Fun's premiere issue were not exactly hilarious. There was a "funny animal" strip called Pelion and Ossa (perhaps the only comic book feature to take its name from mountains that figure in Greek mythology), Caveman Capers, and a college humor strip called Jigger and Ginger. Artist Jack Warren, who had an appealing style but a not very inventive comic mind, was represented by Loco Luke, a cowboy page. Bert Whitman, who'd be a name to reckon with in the comic books of the early 1940s, drew a page featuring a character called Judge Perkins.

Tom McNamara, a veteran newspaper cartoonist, was cartoon editor on the early issues of *New Fun*. His own work was represented by a kid page called *After School*, which was similar to the *Us Boys* strip he'd done for Hearst in the teens and twenties. McNamara's success with *Us Boys* had earned him an invitation from movie producer Hal Roach to participate in the creation of the Our Gang series of two-reel comedies in the early twenties. Working for Roach director-general Charley Chase, McNamara wrote and illustrated title cards and even directed a few of the earliest shorts in the series. Unfortunately, a serious drinking problem reduced him to scuffling for cartoon work by the time Major Nicholson sent out his call.

For a topper to his kid page, McNamara added *My Grandpa*. Drawn in kid style, this was supposed to be a boy cartoonist's account of his grandfather's wild and wooly youthful adventures. McNamara later drew a similar strip, called *Grandpa Peters*, for various DC comics in the early 1940s. In all versions, it was quiet but genuinely funny.

Because of the shaky state of Nicholson's finances, he often didn't get around to paying his artists the small fees—usually five dollars a page—he'd promised them. Besides considerable ill will, this produced noticeable staff turnover. Lyman Anderson quit and was replaced by fellow pulp illustrator W. C. Brigham; Lariar left and Leo O'Mealia eventually inherited characters *Barry O'Neill* and Fang Gow; Barreaux gave way to Monroe Eisenberg.

New artists and writers were also lured into the fold. Vincent Sullivan started by doing a cartoony kid adventure page called *Spike Spalding* and Whitney Ellsworth contributed an *Orphan Annie* imitation named *Little Linda*. Contributions began coming in over the transom, too. From Cleveland came material created by a pair of youngsters named Jerry Siegel and Joe Shuster. The first feature of theirs to see print was *Doctor Occult*, which started in *New Fun* #6 (October 1935). The youthful partners signed the strip with the pen names Leger and Reuths. Dr. Occult, a ghost detective who "has sworn to combat supernatural evil in the world," gets right down to business. In the very first panel, "while passing an alley one evening," he runs into a tuxedo-clad vampire about to siphon some blood from his latest victim. Occult uses a magic symbol to scare the fiend away.

One of the reasons Major Nicholson was having money troubles was that his new magazine simply wasn't selling. The comic book boom hadn't yet begun when he first offered *New Fun* to the world in 1935. In fact, the only other comic book on the newsstands was the fledgling *Famous Funnies*. Distributors were still reluctant to handle comic books and newsstands were even more reluctant to give them valuable rack space. Tom McNamara once recalled that Nicholson's Fourth Avenue loft was usually piled high with unsold, returned copies.

By 1936, as already noted, *Popular*, *Tip Top*, *King*, and *The Funnies* would all be in business. They, of course, all offered reprints of popular, well-established newspaper comics. The major, on the other hand, was trying to gain a foothold with a tabloid-size magazine full of unknown characters. A stubborn, if not overly practical man, he held on.

The sixth issue of the struggling magazine was cover-dated October 1935 and the seventh January 1936—a long time between issues for a comic book that was trying to build an audience and pass itself off as a monthly. In the interval it had shrunk in trim size, moving closer to the comic-book standard. It had also changed its name to *More Fun*. Color had been added and, as it entered its second year of life, the comic looked fairly presentable. The major and his editors, by this time Whitney Ellsworth and Vincent

Artist and writer Tom McNamara had worked on Hal Roach's Our Gang movie shorts in the early 1920s. *New Fun* ran McNamara's *After School* feature a decade later. Here, childlike mischief escalates into a battle of the sexes.

A pair of youngers from Cleveland, Ohio—writer Jerry Siegel and artist Joe Shuster—created character Dr. Occult for *New Fun*. By the time these panels appeared in 1937, Siegel and Shuster were struggling to sell another of their creations: Superman.

Sullivan, promoted the magazine's new look and title by utilizing the venerable advertising gambit of making liabilities seem like assets and differences seem like strengths. The leadoff page in their first standard-size issue, after explaining that the magazine had changed because "so many people wrote in asking for *More Fun* in a smaller, handier size," went on to extol the book's virtues. One was that "everything between these covers is BRAND NEW, never before published," and another was the fact that "all the pictures, type, and lettering are clear and legible . . . no eyestrain."

The magazine now appeared much less like a compilation of rejected newspaper Sundays. Most of the strips filled two pages, usually of six panels each. The straight features outnumbered the humorous ones and just about every adventure strip ended with the words "to be continued." Some of the characters from *New Fun* were still kicking, including *Sandra of the Secret Service*, *Don Drake*, and *Little Linda*. Siegel and Shuster were continuing their *Doctor Occult* and had added *Henri Duval*, a musketeer saga starring a fellow who closely resembled the creators' boyhood idol, Douglas Fairbanks, Sr.

Red-headed hero *Barry O'Neill* was keeping up his battle with the Chinese villain Fang Gow, who also was known as "the inscrutable and vengeful enemy of the human race." Leo O'Mealia, who was rendering O'Neill's adventures, was in his fifties at the time and a veteran of several decades as a newspaper strip artist. He drew this Yellow Peril epic in a meticulous, melodramatic style perfectly suited to its flamboyant plots and prose. No stranger to sinister Orientals, O'Mealia had drawn the *Fu Manchu* newspaper strip that had had a modest two-year run in the early 1930s. He'd obtained further practice at depicting fog-shrouded streets and master villains when he drew the even less successful *Sherlock Holmes* comic strip in 1930. For *More Fun* O'Mealia also produced *Bob Merritt and His Flying Pals*. Handsome, clean-cut Bob was described as a "gentleman adventurer and inventor." If O'Mealia was getting only five dollars per page, he did an impressive amount of pen work to earn it.

Features came and went, as did cartoonists. Alex Blum took over *Ivanhoe*; an artist calling himself Sven Elven carried on *Treasure Island* and added *The Three Musketeers*; Siegel and Shuster abandoned *Henri Duval* for a new cops and robbers strip, *Radio Squad*. Tom Hickey assumed the drawing of *Wing Brady* and a science fiction tale called *Brad Hardy*.

Creig Flessel began working for *More Fun* with issue #12 (August 1936). In his middle twenties, he had been doing illustrations for pulp magazines for the

Leo O'Mealia had illustrated the *Fu Manchu* newspaper strip in the early 1930s and was known for his deftness in drawing the "sinister Oriental" stereotype popular at the time. In this 1937 Bob Merritt page that ran in *More Fun*, our hero is at the mercy of some "silent Asiatics."

past two years. Flessel had heard about the major's comic book activities by way of an ad in the *New York Times*. He remembers that Nicholson had "a continental air. Spats, a cane, a beaver hat, cigarette holder clenched between rotten teeth. He always bowed when he shook hands with you." Flessel drew *Pep Morgan*, about a college athlete, and *The Bradley Boys*, concerning two youths roughing it in the wilderness. He also began doing covers. A polished artist even then, Flessel displayed a slickness that many of his contemporaries lacked.

By the spring of 1937, *More Fun* was running fewer features but daring to innovate by giving most strips four entire pages. All of the adventure features continued, but each hero and heroine had been given more room to move around in. Because the major couldn't afford full color throughout, a dozen of his sixty-four pages were black and white, and another eight were three-color: black, white, and red. The December 1937 issue offered an eight-page western yarn titled *The Ucca Terror*. It was drawn by Homer Fleming, another veteran cartoonist, and was a complete, self-contained story. From then on, four-, six-, and eight-page stories dominated *More Fun*.

Undaunted by the lack of success of his tabloid-sized *New Fun* Comics, the intrepid Major Nicholson added a second magazine, *New Comics*, late in 1935. In shape, size, and general appearance, the premiere issue was close to what would become the standard format for comic books, except that *New Comics* contained eighty pages, sixteen more than the usual amount, and had an uncoated, non-glossy paper cover. Like its predecessor, the new comic book was not full color throughout, and offered a hodgepodge of adventure and comedy strips, and a variety of text

PEP HURTLES HEAD OVER HEELS DOWN A 20 FOOT BANK—LANDING RIGHT SIDE UP.!!!—

THE FINISH! PEP IS UNABLE TO OVERTAKE THE WINNER—BUT FINISHES SECOND GIVING HIS TEAM THE NEEDED 3 POINTS TO WIN THE MEET.

College athlete Pep Morgan takes a tough fall in a 1937 *More Fun* adventure with art by Creig Fessel.

©1937 by DC Comics, Inc.

Hero Barry O'Neill works to thwart the evil Fang Gow with artwork by Leo O'Mealia.   ©1937 by DC Comics, Inc.

features. As the title evolved, adventure fans could enjoy *Castaway Island*, *Slim and Tex*, *Captain Quick*, *Dale Daring*, and *Federal Men*. On the light side were strips like *Dickie Duck*, *Sagebrush N' Cactus*, and *J. Worthington Blimp, Esq.* The obligatory text story often ran to six pages or more and there were columns devoted to radio, movies, puzzles, book reviews, magic tricks, cartooning tips, and letters from readers— "Marjorie Callaghan of 584 4th St., Brooklyn, says that getting a copy of NEW COMICS is like buying all the Sunday papers in the city just for the funnies, except that you get more in NEW COMICS."

New Comics was dubbed the "international picture story magazine" by its enterprising publisher. Included among the staffers responsible for living up to this lofty claim were business manager John Mahon and managing editor William Cook; Vincent Sullivan was initially assistant editor. Cook and Mahon, as we'll see, soon defected to start a comic book of their own. With the sixth issue, *New Comics* dropped to sixty-four pages and with the seventh started using heavier stock for covers.

The dynamic duo from Cleveland, Siegel and Shuster, came up with another feature, *Federal Men*, which ▶

Malcolm Wheeler-Nicholson

Perhaps the most colorful figure in comic book history is Major Malcolm Wheeler-Nicholson, a onetime cavalry officer and prolific adventure writer who became one of the first moguls of the comic book industry.

©1930 by Argosy

Born in 1890, Malcolm Wheeler-Nicholson was at various times in his life a major in the U.S. Army cavalry, a fairly successful writer of action and adventure yarns for pulp-fiction magazines, and a not-so-successful publisher of comic books. Dapper and well-groomed, he had an erect military bearing, carried a cane, and wore spats. "I was born in the South," he once explained, "raised on a western ranch, worked for a while as a cub newspaper reporter, became a second lieutenant of cavalry in the regular army, chased bandits on the Mexican border, fought fevers and played polo in the Philippines, led a battalion of infantry against the Bolsheviki in Siberia, helped straighten out the affairs of the army in France, commanded the headquarters cavalry of the American force in the Rhine, and left the army as a major equipped with a select assortment of racing and polo cups, a saber, and a battered typewriter."

Nicholson's parting with the service in the early 1920s was not an especially amicable one. An outspoken fellow, he'd made an assortment of charges against his senior officers and gone so far as to accuse them of Prussianism. These charges he also put into a letter to President Harding. That caused him considerable discomfort in the form of various charges brought against him by the army. It wasn't until 1924, after hearings and countercharges and threats of lawsuits by Nicholson, that the controversy ended. Nicholson, who'd already written professionally on military matters, took up that battered typewriter and embarked on a career as a writer of fiction. He was soon selling to many of the most popular pulps, especially to *Adventure and Argosy*. His specialties were stories of military action around the world and historical tales of intrigue and swordplay. His was a name that editors would showcase on their covers.

After the major was eased out of the comic book company he had founded, he returned to the writing of both fiction and nonfiction. He gradually dropped from sight and died in 1968.

Tarzan, created by novelist Edgar Rice Burroughs, was wildly popular and inspired countless comic book imitators. One of them was a jungle lord named Sandor who had been raised by wild dogs. His adventures, drawn by Homer Fleming, appeared in *New Comics*.

began in *New Comics* #2 (January 1936). This was a serial strip starring Steve Carson, whose grim, sharp-featured profile probably made even Dick Tracy envious. Almost from the start, the young writer-artist team, unlike most of their peers, encouraged reader response to their feature. At the conclusion of the four-page episode in issue #3 they promised a "FREE original drawing of Steve Carson along with a personal message" to the fan who sent in "the most interesting and constructive letter." The magazine's fifth issue brought the Junior Federal Men Club; there was no charge to join at first, but dues eventually were set at a dime.

Very soon in *Federal Men* Siegel and Shuster betrayed the fact that they were longtime science fiction enthusiasts. After introducing a gang of villains who operated a mysterious submarine, they tweaked the plot to include a criminal invasion of Washington, D.C. with a gigantic tank. Next came a mammoth robot, a metal colossus built along the lines of King Kong—"Populace Terrified by Nightmarish Invader!" Steve Carson helps defeat "the scientific criminals who sought to capture America," and then it was back to machine guns and dope rings for a while.

Since the major's fondness for classics, and near classics, hadn't abated, *New Comics* offered an adaptation of Dickens's *A Tale of Two Cities* in two-page doses, from #4 onward. Commencing in #6, H. Rider Haggard's *She*, illustrated by Sven Elven, was serialized. More cultural uplift was provided by an adaptation of the King Arthur legend and a long-running Viking saga.

Comic books' first Tarzan impersonator appeared in *New Comics* #5. By the time the character, Sandor, set up shop in the jungle, the choices for animal surrogate parents had become restricted—other jungle heroes had been raised by apes, wolves, tigers, and lions. "In the deep jungles of Northern India lives a strange white youth known as Sandor," the copy gamely explained, "raised from infancy by a pack of wild dogs that now acknowledge him as their leader." Despite his humble up-bringing, the golden-skinned Sandor did a commendable job as "the deadly enemy of Rajah Marajah, ruler of the people of the Lost Civilization." Homer Fleming was the artist.

Issue #5 also brought the debut of *Steve Conrad*. Nicely drawn by Creig Flessel, the initial episodes were printed in black and white. Steve, described as an "adventurer, scientist and inventor of the Cyanogen Cruiser," was involved in exploring Dolorosa Isle, "a tropical island with a mountain range, treach-erous swamps, dense jungles, and an abundance of vegetation . . . it is not inhabited by man or beast!" That initial appraisal of real estate conditions on Dolorosa proved to be wildly inaccurate and soon Steve and his comrades, including a pretty blonde stowaway named Myrna, were up to their elbows in murderous savages and an evil ruler known as the Great Devachan. When color was added to the strip a few issues later, readers were unsettled to discover that most of the natives of the isle were a bright green.

The best funny material in the first issues of *New* was supplied by teenage Brooklyn cartoonist Sheldon Mayer. When asked how he first got together with the major, he replied, "I just walked into the office, because I saw the stuff on the newsstands and I wrote down the addresses. I'd been doing that all along with all sorts of things." Even though Major Nicholson never paid him, Mayer has said, "You couldn't hate him. He was a charmer." After showing his samples and getting an okay to do some features, the boy cartoonist asked if he might have a small advance with which to buy bristol board, ink, and other supplies. The major promptly wrote out a check for one dollar. When Mayer asked Cook and Mahon where he might cash it, Mahon took the check from him and handed him a dollar from his own pocket. Mayer has always believed the dollar was one that had come in from a reader that day for a subscription.

Mayer drew two features, both adapted from unsold newspaper strip ideas. *J. Worthington Blimp, Esq.*, as its title suggests, starred a plump windbag of a fellow who shared some of the attributes of W. C. Fields and

Popeye's chum Wimpy. The continuity had to do with Blimp's attempts to cross the country on a bicycle. The strip had some of the freewheeling and rowdy flavor of Billy DeBeck's *Barney Google*. In the other feature, *The Strange Adventures of Mr. Weed*, Mayer played with fantasy and time travel. Weed is a scholarly young fellow who teams up with a plump inventor to journey back to 1835 in a time machine the inventor has put together in his basement. The stories and dialogue in both strips were bright and Mayer, even at eighteen, was drawing like a pro.

With the twelfth issue *New Comics* became *New Adventure Comics*. For years one of the best markets for Major Nicholson's fiction had been the prestigious pulp *Adventure*, whose untrimmed pages he shared with Talbot Mundy, Harold Lamb, and scores of other top-rank pulp-fiction writers. Nicholson borrowed the successful pulp's name for his struggling comic, which soon began to transform itself. The most

obvious change occurred on the cover. The word *New* waned and slid over to the far left; *Adventure* became dominant. The earliest covers that came after the name change were whimsical instead of flat-out funny. Less than ten issues later, though, dramatic action became the predominant cover element.

During its second year, *New Adventure* overhauled its interior, as well. While almost all the adventure features were carried on, they now filled from four to eight pages as opposed to the mere two favored earlier. In 1938 the magazine grew even more action oriented, and after #31 (October 1938) *New* was dropped from the logo entirely; with the next issue the magazine became simply *Adventure Comics*, signaling the beginning of one of the longest-running titles in comic book history.

Another long-lived title, and the cornerstone of the DC empire, is *Detective Comics*, which got off to a modest start early in 1937. This was the last title the enterprising but underfunded Major Nicholson had his name attached to. The premiere issue was dated March 1937, and sported a cover featuring a sinister-looking Oriental, who glowers at the reader from against a crimson background. The new title had been hyped in December 1936 issues of Nicholson's other two titles, in ads that promised that *Detective Comics*

was going to be "the most thrilling narrative-cartoon magazine in the comic field." The major's financial problems, however, were worsening and publication was delayed three months.

It was at about this time that Harry Donenfeld became more actively involved with Nicholson. An aggressive and gregarious man in his late thirties, Donenfeld had been involved in several aspects of the magazine business for most of the decade. He published pulp magazines under several company names and was a partner in the Independent News Company distribution operation. He also owned the printing plant that ran off covers for Major Nicholson's comics. Nicholson, who owed money for those covers, had also been advanced funds from Donenfeld's distribution wing. In order to get *Detective* launched, Nicholson was obliged to take on Donenfeld as a partner.

A new company was formed to publish the latest title—Detective Comics, Inc.—and its owners were listed as Nicholson and J. S. Liebowitz. Liebowitz was Donenfeld's accountant. Contrary to most previously published accounts, Nicholson stayed on with *Detective Comics* throughout its entire first year and didn't give it up, along with his other titles, until 1938. Vincent Sullivan served as editor of *Detective*. A former newspaper sports cartoonist, he'd been with the major's shaky organization from almost the start. When asked many years later if he'd drawn that first cover of the magazine, he replied that he was pretty sure he had, since he'd been fascinated with the Fu Manchu brand of villainy at that time.

As implied by the comic's title, the initial issue featured nothing but detectives—more than a half dozen of them plus humorous fillers dealing with mystery and sleuthing.

Like the pulp detective fiction magazines and the movies that inspired it, *Detective Comics* dished out plenty of action, suspense, and violence. Many of the stories attempted formal mystery plotting, offering an array of suspects and clues. There was a little bit of everything, from tough cop to dapper amateur investigator. Speed Saunders, a plainclothes cop who covered the waterfront, occupied the leadoff spot. He was a clean-cut fellow with a fondness for trenchcoats. When the able Creig Flessel gave up the ace investigator in the spring of 1938, Fred Guardineer took over the drawing and Gardner Fox the scripting. Speed became tougher, abandoned the waterfront, and took to wearing plaid suits. His cases grew more violent and sometimes became downright gruesome.

Major Nicholson himself wrote the adventures of Brad Nelson, the "crack amateur sleuth" whose first adventure was entitled "The Claws of the Red Dragon." The storyline went on for eight issues and involved Nelson with unscrupulous Orientals, a lovely blonde, and a great deal of violence. Later Nelson cases included "The Blood of the Lotus," "Murder in the Clouds," and "The Song of Death." Tom Hickey, a disciple of newspaper-strip stars Alex Raymond and Milton Caniff, supplied the artwork.

An even suaver detective was Cosmo, also known as the Phantom of Disguise. He was a handsome fellow who solved cases all over the world. When the Manhattan police or the best brains of Scotland Yard were baffled, they turned to him— "Ah! Cosmo! Why didn't I think of him before? Let's call him in!" And for readers who liked a touch of sagebrush in their mysteries, the magazine offered Buck Marshall, who was a range detective by trade.

Although stuck at the tail end of the first issue, the closest thing to a star that *Detective* had was Slam Bradley. Billed as an "ace freelance sleuth, fighter and adventurer," he was another Siegel and Shuster creation. Slam's first case involved him in mystery and murder in the bowels of Chinatown. As his name suggests, Slam was a rough and tumble operative who used his fists more often than he used a magnifying glass. He owed as much to Roy Crane's freewheeling soldier of fortune, Captain Easy, as he did to the private eyes of pulps and movies. And just as Easy had the diminutive Wash Tubbs as a sidekick, Slam had Shorty Morgan. They teamed up, after a considerable show of reluctance on Slam's part, during the first case.

Unlike many fictional private detectives, Slam rarely used a gun, relying instead on his fists and his nerve to arrive at a solution. One early investigation begins with his chasing a suspect circus performer right up onto the fellow's trapeze, another with Slam crashing through a roof after a parachute jump. He and Shorty solved crimes and misdemeanors in Hollywood, on Broadway, in Mexico, and the frozen North. Deeply enamored of science fiction, Siegel and Shuster eventually involved Slam and Shorty with rocket ships, magic, and even time travel. And it was on this feature that the creative team began experimenting with the use of full-page splash panels at a time when most comic book layouts were still as sedate as those of newspaper Sunday pages.

Spy was another Siegel & Shuster creation. The initial episode, which looks as though it was made up from unsold Sunday pages, introduced Bart Regan and his fiancee, Sally Norris. Working together each month in the give-and-take manner of Nick and Nora Charles in the Thin Man movies, the couple led

As this *New Comics* ad explained, the comic was fun to read and healthful, too—adapted newspaper-comic reprints were often reduced in size, forcing editors to squash or rewrite the text. Original comics had no such growing (or shrinking!) pains. Art is by Vincent Sullivan.

a fast-paced life in locations around the world while combating spies, saboteurs, and other enemies of Uncle Sam.

Despite its emphasis on detectives, *Detective Comics* wasn't all gloom and violence; quite a bit of comic crimebusting was going on, too. Sullivan and Whit Ellsworth, a co-editor on early issues, provided pages of gag cartoons. During the magazine's second years, cartoonist Bob Kane (remember that name) began a one-page filler featuring Oscar the Gumshoe.

The most sinister Oriental of all time set up shop in *Detective* #18 (July 1938). Departing from its policy of using only original material, the magazine began reprinting the *Fu Manchu* newspaper strip. This heady blend of Yellow Peril melodrama and flowery romance vanished after issue #27.

Detective got its first costumed hero in issue #20. The Crimson Avenger owed a great deal to a hero of another color, the Green Hornet. The Hornet had first taken to the air over Detroit's radio station WXYZ in 1936, and by the spring of 1938 was being heard nationwide on the Mutual radio network. Whereas the Hornet was Britt Reid, daring young publisher of the *Daily Sentinel*, the Crimson Avenger was Lee Travis, daring young publisher of the *Globe Leader*. The only person who knew the Hornet's true identity was his faithful valet, Kato. The Crimson Avenger's secret was shared only by his Chinese servant, Wing. Like the Hornet, the Crimson Avenger never used a deadly weapon, preferring instead to put his adversaries to sleep with a blast from his gas gun. As drawn by Jim Chambers, he wore a dark blue slouch hat, a domino mask, and a crimson, Inverness-style cape. Much flashier than the private eyes and cops with whom he shared the magazine, the Crimson Avenger had a moment of stardom when he was featured on the cover of *Detective* #22. Unfortunately for him, a new and more original costumed hero came along a few issues later. We'll talk more about this new character in Chapter 5.

As noted earlier, William Cook had worked briefly as managing editor on *New Fun* in 1935. In 1936 he and John Mahon, another defector from Major Nicholson's camp, formed the Comics Magazine Company, Inc. Their first title was *The Comics Magazine* (within a few months it became Funny Pages), and had a May 1936 cover date on the debut issue. Cook and Mahon promised their readers that everything was original and new and that "the creators of the features in this issue have established themselves with fans in all parts of the world." The early issues offered the same mixture of adventure and comedy as the major's magazines. In fact, some of the strips were unpublished *New Fun* and *New Comics* material. Sheldon Mayer was there with two strips, Siegel and Shuster's Dr. Occult was practicing his ghost detecting as Dr. Mystic, and *New Comics'* *Federal Men* feature was altered and issued as *Federal Agent*. Later in 1936, *Funny Picture Stories* appeared, promising "Mystery Thriller, Ace Adventure, Western," and introducing George Brenner's character, the Clock, the first mystery man in comics.

The Clock was a natty fellow who did his detecting in tuxedo and gray fedora. He covered his face with a black silken mask and carried a gold-headed cane. Brenner, who wrote and drew the feature, was quite probably influenced by Leslie Charteris's Saint as well as by such dapper pulp crime fighters as the Phantom Detective. Just as the Saint left behind a card adorned with a haloed stick figure, The Clock left a card with the depiction of a timepiece and the slogan *The Clock Has Struck.*

Detective Picture Stories was the next offering from Comics Magazine Company, and was devoted to the single theme of crime detection. "Here is a magazine crammed full of color, action, plot and punch," promised a subscription ad. "You'll see why crime does not pay, why the police always put the finger on the criminal." The stories were longer than those in the Nicholson magazines, up to ten pages, and all were self-contained. There were no regularly featured "star" detectives. Story titles were reminiscent of those in pulp magazines: "Murder in the Blue Room," "The Diamond Dick," "The Phantom Killer." Among the artists were Bert Christman, Ed Moore, and George Brenner. Although the first issue's cover promised a Clock story, none showed up inside. The fourth issue contained *Muss 'em Up*, an early effort by writer-artist Will Eisner.

Despite a line of three titles, Cook and Mahon did not do well. By the middle of 1937 they had sold out to an outfit called Ultem Publications. Ultem in turn sold its interests the following year to Joseph Hardie, who made the magazines the basis of his Centaur Publications, Inc. *Detective Picture Stories* became *Keen Detective Funnies* (a snappy title!) in the summer of 1938. Lloyd Jacquet, another Nicholson alum, was the editor. The retitled magazine's first star was the Clock. Of the sleuths who appeared in support, a character with one foot in the costumed-adventurer camp was the Masked Marvel. Most of *Keen's* other detectives were more prosaic. These included Thurston Hunt, Terry Taylor, and Rock Baird. In the sixth issue a scientific sleuth named Dean Denton joined the lineup.

Over time, a variety of detective characters continued to check in and out of the magazine. There were Stony Dawson, TNT Todd of the FBI, and Little Dynamite. This last one was the first adventure feature by artist Jack Cole to see print—Cole would go on to do brilliantly clever work in the forties and fifties.

A farsighted entrepreneur named Harry "A" Chesler was one of the first to suspect that there was going to be a comic book industry in America. His initial by the way, didn't stand for anything and was stuck into the middle of his name and set off by quotes for no other reason than Chesler liked the way it looked. In 1936 Harry "A", who neither drew nor wrote, opened an office at 276 Fifth Avenue in Manhattan and set up what was the first comic art shop. Hiring artists and writers who'd work cheaply, he began to produce features for the original-material comic magazines. The field being what it was at the time, the pioneering shop initially had only two customers—Major Nicholson and the renegade Cook-Mahon outfit. Late in 1936 Chesler decided to branch out into publishing and the result was two new titles, *Star Comics* and *Star Ranger*, both cover-dated February 1937. These were initially slightly larger than their newsstand rivals, measuring 8 inches by 11, but running just forty-eight pages.

Star Comics offered a blend of adventure and humor features, most of them one to three pages in length. The exceptions were *Dan Hastings*, which went to eight, and *The Mad Goddess*, which came in at seven. The *Hastings* opus was laid out in Sunday-page style and bears a 1935 copyright date, indicating that Chesler had made an unsuccessful attempt to peddle it as a newspaper feature. A science fiction adventure, *Dan Hastings*, was first drawn by Clemens Gretter and carried on by Fred Guardineer.

The Mad Goddess was set "in the jungles of South America," and drawn by Robert L. Golden.

It was billed as "a complete adventure story." Other artists in the first issue were Creig Flessel, Fred Schwab, Henry C. Kiefer, and Dick Moores, who was represented by *King Kole's Court*, another unsold Sunday page. Moores eventually took over the *Gasoline Alley* newspaper strip.

Star Ranger, filled entirely with cowboys, both serious and whimsical, was the first comic book devoted entirely to the West. Ken Fitch served as editor and wrote many of the stories. Several prolific pulp-fiction writers also got credits, including Norman Daniels and Tom Curry. Among the early artists were Flessel, Guardineer, Schwab, and Rafael Astarita.

After publishing a half dozen issues of each of the magazines, Chesler sold them. Eventually they came under Joseph Hardie's Centaur banner. *Star Comics* continued to concentrate on short material, an average issue containing as many as three dozen different features. Among the other contributors were artists Jack Cole, Ken Ernst, Bob Wood, and Charles Biro. Robert Winsor McCay, signing himself Winsor McCay, Jr., revived his father's best-known creation and drew some sadly uninspired *Little Nemo* pages for the magazine. In its latter-day issues *Star Comics* included Tarpé Mills's *Diana Dean in Hollywood*, Paul Gustavson's *Speed Silvers*, and Carl Burgos's *The Last Pirate*. All of these artists went on to better things.

Star Comics survived for twenty-three issues before expiring in the summer of 1939. *Star Ranger*, after undergoing a couple of title changes (*Cowboy Comics*, followed by *Star Ranger Funnies*), folded in the fall of the same year.

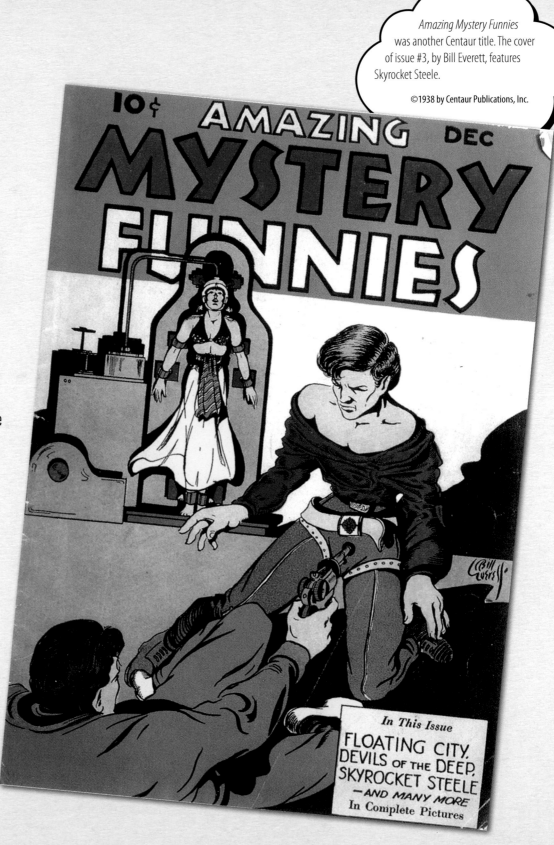

Amazing Mystery Funnies was another Centaur title. The cover of issue #3, by Bill Everett, features Skyrocket Steele.

©1938 by Centaur Publications, Inc.

CHAPTER 4

Heroes For Sale

The original-material comic books gradually moved away from imitating the look of their reprint rivals. In addition to fewer panels per page, Major Nicholson and his followers came increasingly to use complete stories and ones that ran from six to eight pages. They also realized the importance of recurring characters in building reader loyalty. Interestingly enough, however, both kinds of early comic books tended to stress the *quantity* of features available and to avoid giving any one character favored treatment.

The reprint titles, such as *Famous Funnies*, *Tip Top*, and *Crackajack*, featured bunches of characters on their covers. *Comics on Parade*, for instance, didn't allow a character to solo on a cover until Li'l Abner was given the nod for the seventh issue. *Ace Comics* didn't disperse the crowds until the cover of the fourteenth issue, when the aggressively nonheroic Katzenjammer Kids began a several-year run as cover boys. During its initial year in business, *New Comics* used only funny covers, most of them drawn by Whit Ellsworth. Issue #15 (May 1937) marked the first time the magazine, now titled *New Adventure*, sported a straight adventure cover. Creig Flessel drew that as well as the next one, which depicted Steve Carson of *Federal Men*. Flessel did the next sixteen covers in a row, none

Comic books did not spring fully formed from a vacuum. Pulp magazines, movie serials, Big Little Books, and other forms of popular entertainment influenced comic books's development. Here, it's cross and doublecross as a trio of miscreants draws the attention of pulp avenger the Black Bat.

©1939 by Better Publications, Inc.

of which made use of any of *Adventure*'s characters. It was not until the advent of Sandman in #40 (July 1939) that a hero from within the magazine showed up again on its front.

Detective Comics followed a similar policy, although all of its covers stressed mystery and action rather than humor. With issue #18 (August 1938), that top-seeded Oriental menace, Fu Manchu, became the first interior character to be shown on a cover. The cover of issue #22 (December 1938) featured the masked crimebuster called the Crimson Avenger, who had the distinction of being the first *Detective hero* to rate a cover.

The situation was no different with DC's competition. For example, Centaur's *Funny Pages* utilized nothing but comedy covers for twenty-nine issues, few of which made use of characters to be found inside the magazine. *Funny Pages* didn't depict a hero, a chap named the Arrow, until the summer of 1939. *Funny Picture Stories* showcased the Clock on the cover of its first issue, then switched to adventure covers that highlighted detectives, explorers, Royal Mounties, and similarly generic heroes. After that came a dozen gag covers.

By imitating the Sunday comic sections and some pulp magazines of the anthology type, such as *Adventure* and *Argosy*, the early comic book titles of the 1930s overlooked two of the basic rules

of catering to a young audience. Namely, that kids like larger-than-life heroes and they don't usually like them in bunches. In time, comic book publishers got the hint, and joined in on the wholesale manufacture of fictional heroes that was already going on in other, competing media.

Fictional heroes had become increasingly accessible to the broad American public in the 19th century. From the early 1800s onward, Americans grew more literate and printing methods became faster and cheaper. As the century progressed, more and more people were able to, and wanted to, read about famous men— politicians, soldiers, and celebrities. Besides stories of real-life men of accomplishment, the unfolding 19th century offered a growing number of made-up heroes. Somewhere in between were larger-than-life figures such as Daniel Boone, Davy Crockett, Kit Carson, and Buffalo Bill, who entered the public consciousness via published adventures that were partly real and a good deal fictitious.

Magazines blossomed and so did inexpensive books; adolescents were especially fond of the many

Man overboard as the Sandman does his bit for justice in 1939.

©1939 by National Periodical Publications, Inc.

A 1915 "dime novel" (of the fifteen–cent variety) featuring hero Nick Carter.

©1915 by Street & Smith Publications, Inc.

five-cent fiction weeklies and the ubiquitous "dime novels." Fictional heroes continued to multiply right on through the end of the 19th century and into the next. Readers responded to figures like Old Sleuth, Frank Reade, Jr., Nick Carter, Frank Merriwell, Deadwood Dick, Young Wild West, and Roaring Ralph Rockwood the Ruthless Ranger.

Gradually, pulp magazines supplanted the dime novels and fiction weeklies. Heroes were plentiful in the pulps. Like the comic books that came later, pulps usually sold for ten cents a copy. They sported colorful, often lurid covers and usually measured 9½ by 7½ inches. Page counts ranged from 114 to 162.

One of the earliest and most influential of the pulp mystery men appeared in 1914 in Street & Smith's *People Magazine*. Jimmie Dale, alias the Gray Seal, was the creation of Canadian author Frank L. Packard. Inspired by such earlier figures as Raffles and Jimmy Valentine, Jimmie Dale did them one better. He had an alternate identity, that of the Gray Seal, a mysterious, masked avenger who prowled the midnight streets of Manhattan. Hunted by the law, yet actually a man dedicated to justice, he struck swiftly and left behind only a small sticker, the notorious gray seal. In the everyday world Jimmie Dale was a wealthy playboy, but he had several other identities as well. "As Larry the Bat, the dope fiend, he slinks through the dens of Chinatown," explained one blurb. "As Smarlinghue, the artist, he cadges beers in the Bowery, and as the Gray Seal . . . he uses clues and tips gathered in these disguises to battle and confound the underworld."

The leading creator of phantom detectives and mystery men was a onetime newspaper reporter

Frank Reade, Jr. hits the jungle trail with his fabulous bicycle car. This adventure was devoured by young readers in 1903.

©1903 by Frank Tousey

from the Midwest named Johnston McCulley. Although he created one of the most famous masked men of the 20th century, McCulley is little remembered and seldom written about. Regardless, McCulley made his mark, for it was in the spring of 1919 that his serial "The Curse of Capistrano" began in Munsey's *All-Story Weekly*. This five-part story introduced Zorro to the world.

While Zorro was McCulley's best-known character and one about whom the ex-newsman wrote more than sixty novels and stories, Zorro was only one of the many dual identity characters McCulley created. He also introduced a hooded villain called Black Star and a mysterious criminal known as the Spider (a very popular name through the years for both heroes and villains). In the 1920s, McCulley created a gallery of masked good guys, including the Thunderbolt, the Man in Purple, and the Crimson Clown.

The most important pulp mystery man of the thirties was the Shadow. His first adventure was published early in 1931, and was the creation of a young man named Walter B. Gibson. Using the pen name Maxwell Grant, Gibson wrote nearly three hundred novels about the scourge of crime over the next two decades. While the Shadow was somewhat similar to earlier pulp avengers, such as Zorro and the Gray Seal, he dressed much more like a sinister villain, in black cloak and slouch hat. His weapons of choice were twin .45 automatics. Several comic book heroes, most notably Batman, would also use their costumes to strike fear into the hearts of their foes. (Interestingly, Batman packed a pistol in his earliest adventures.)

The Shadow was not an easy man to get to know. In the first novels, in fact, even Gibson didn't seem quite sure who the Shadow was. Unlike the Jimmie Dale novels, there were no interludes in the Shadow stories that showed the real Shadow relaxing with friends before slipping into a disguise. The Shadow never appeared before the reader undisguised. Often he lurked in the background, emulating the sinister menace of a horror film. He had a love of obfuscation and dim lighting and came across as a man who would wear a mask even when he's alone in a pitch black room.

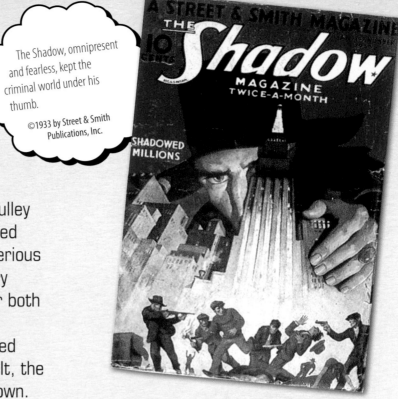

The Shadow, omnipresent and fearless, kept the criminal world under his thumb.

©1933 by Street & Smith Publications, Inc.

Above: The crimefighting Spider spins his web on the cover of his first issue.

©1933 by Popular Publications

Right: The pulps did not shy away from gore, as this 1938 *Spider* cover attests.

©1938 by Popular Publications

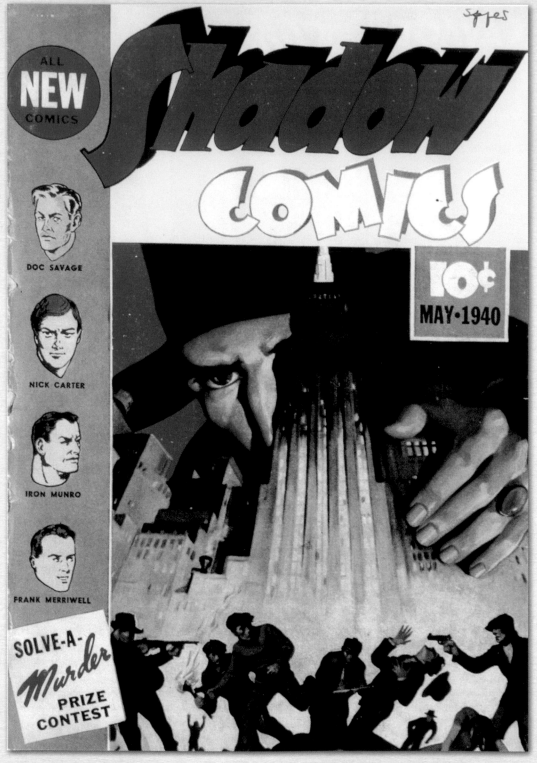

The early Shadow stories were heavy with disappearances, fireworks, surprises, and mysterious atmosphere. The Shadow novels, especially those of the early 1930s, were usually about the people the character worked through, the crooks he destroyed, and the agents he manipulated. Gradually the Shadow acquired an assortment of alter egos that opened up the stories and gave the character more room to move about. His best-known pseudo-identity was that of Lamont Cranston, millionaire playboy. He was also fond of appearing as Fritz, the janitor at police headquarters. Eventually, in the late thirties, it was revealed that the Shadow was actually a noted aviator named Kent Allard, though by that time most readers thought he was actually Lamont Cranston.

Street & Smith, publisher of *The Shadow*, scored again in 1933 with *Doc Savage*. The brilliant, overpoweringly strong Doc—known to all as the Man of Bronze—was to have a considerable influence on the development of Superman. Quick-witted, muscular, and physically fearless, Doc had devoted his life to "striving to help those who needed it, punishing those who deserved it." Unlike the Shadow, Doc was not a killer but a nobler, less frightening figure. Written by Lester Dent under the pseudonym Kenneth Robeson, the Doc Savage adventures were frequently science-fictional and filled with outlandish gadgets—futuristic weapons or tools that Doc could count on to get him out of tight spots.

Doc and the Shadow—each defining "hero" in a way completely different from the other—were perhaps the preeminent pulp heroes. Most of the other successful pulp heroes of the decade fell into the mystery man category. These included the Spider and the Phantom Detective, both of whom began to stalk and fight crime in 1933. Secret Agent X first showed

Cover art from the January 1, 1933 issue of the Shadow pulp (page 51, top right) was recycled seven years later for the Shadow comic book.

©1933, 1940 by Street & Smith Publications, Inc.

Pulp hero Doc Savage, seen here on the cover of a 1935 issue of his magazine, strongly influenced the creators of Superman.

©1935 by Street & Smith Productions, Inc.

The Shadow preferred to dole out justice from unexpected hiding places.

©1933 by Street & Smith Productions, Inc.

The well-heeled pulp hero known as the Phantom Detective spends a day at the races in 1946.

©1946 by Standard Magazines, Inc.

up on the scene (in disguise) in 1934. His "ability as an impersonator is a combination of superlative voice mimicry, character acting that great Thespians might well envy, and a sculptor-like skill in modeling plastic material over his own features so that they resemble those of another man." The Whisperer came along in 1936 and the Avenger in 1939. Finally, in 1940, the Green Lama arrived.

Most of the mysterious avengers of the pulps, except for Secret Agent X, had alternate civilian identities. An unusually large percentage were wealthy, big-city playboys. Not surprisingly, per-

haps, a great many comic book crimefighters and superheroes would be recruited from the playboy class. Other elements of the pulp hero milieu that were carried over into comics were the Criminal Mastermind and the Fiendish Plot. The Shadow contended, for instance, with recurring villains like the notorious Voodoo Master and the sinister Shiwan Khan. The Spider had to deal with such problems as "a city swept by Bubonic Plague"; with an epidemic that turns America's finest families into a "set of swanky thieves and killers"; with the Emperor of Hades, who "scattered

his scarlet, slaying devil-dust" over Manhattan; with five thousand mad dogs who go on a rampage in Cologne, Ohio (!); and with dozens of equally unsettling villains and situations. Doc Savage had his hands full, too: He met the Thousand Headed Man, the Red Skull, the Thing that Pursued, and others.

Such carryings-on were the stuff of vivid, highly salable adventure, so the pulp fiction magazines did not hesitate to frequently feature a leading hero on a cover, or to devote an entire magazine to a single character. But comic books, as noted earlier, were slow to follow.

The *Whisperer*, the alter ego of police commissioner "Wildcat" Gordon, first appeared as a backup feature in the *Shadow* pulp before spinning off with his first solo issue (pictured).

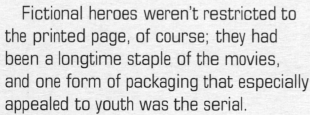

©1936 by Street & Smith Productions, Inc.

The Black Bat gets the dropp on a killer in this gory *Black Book Detective* pulp cover from 1939.

©1939 by Better Publications, Inc.

The Masked Detective, here outfitted with a pith helmet and .45 automatic for an adventure in the Canal Zone, was a particularly rugged pulp hero.

©1942 by Better Publications, Inc.

Fictional heroes weren't restricted to the printed page, of course; they had been a longtime staple of the movies, and one form of packaging that especially appealed to youth was the serial.

These "continued-next-week" chapter plays had started showing up in movie theaters during the second decade of the 20th century. Many of the earliest cliffhangers were built around the exploits of heroines—*The Adventures of Kathlyn*, *The Perils of Pauline*, *The Hazards of Helen*, *The Exploits of Elaine*, and other silent serials tickled audiences with edge-of-the-seat predicaments of beautiful, daring women.

Serials quickly grew in popularity; film historian Alan G. Barbour estimates that more than 250 of them were released between 1913 and 1930. During the thirties, an era that saw the advent of the double bill and the flourishing of the Saturday and Sunday matinee, serials continued to be an important Hollywood product. In that decade well over a hundred sound serials were produced. They ran from twelve to fifteen chapters, with each chapter lasting about fifteen to twenty minutes. In order to follow a 1930s serial hero from his first moment of peril to the final unmasking of the villain a kid had to attend every weekend matinee at the local movie house for three to four months—a pretty long time to be kept in suspense!

Movie screens overflowed with serial heroes of every stripe and job description. Cowboys were popular and often were played by B-movie favorites such as Tim McCoy, Tom Mix, Buck Jones, and Gene Autry. There were also explorers, wonder dogs, G-Men, aviators, Marines, and Royal Canadian Mounted Policemen.

The mask was an important chapter play prop, useful to both bad guys and good guys. Included among the masked crimefighters were the Phantom Rider, Zorro, the Lone Ranger, the Copperhead, the Green Hornet, The Shadow, and the Spider. These last two, of course, were adapted from the pulps.

Several serials were inspired by the exploits of newspaper-strip heroes. Flash Gordon and Buck Rogers, both played by Buster Crabbe, were featured in successful movie cliffhangers, as were Dick Tracy, Tailspin Tommy, Don Winslow, Secret Agent X-9, and Mandrake the Magician.

Moviemakers weren't the only ones to take an increased interest in kids during the 1930s. Advertisers, too, saw dollar signs when they looked at youngsters. The favored medium for reaching them during this Depression decade was radio. In those long ago years radio provided much more than just the music and information that are staples of today's broadcasts. There was also an infinite variety of drama and comedy.

A great many radio programs were designed to appeal to children and many of these were built around adventure heroes. The shows, usually in a serial format and aired five times a week in fifteen-minute segments, were heard

One thin dime bought pulp readers the latest Doc Savage adventure, touted here by a 1934 advertisement.

©1934 by Street & Smith Publications, Inc.

Olympic swimming champion Larry "Buster" Crabbe (second from right) became a Hollywood star when he played the lead in three *Flash Gordon* serials. These lively and fun chapter plays remain popular today.

©1936 by Universal Pictures

chiefly during the children's hour. That was a period that might start as early as 4:30 in the afternoon and run as late as 6:00. Just as women's daytime serials were sponsored primarily by the makers of soap and other domestic products, the kids' serials were sponsored by breakfast-food manufacturers and other makers of things to eat and drink.

Among the earliest kid radio serials were *Skippy*, *Little Orphan Annie* —both adapted from newspaper comics—and *The Air Adventures of Jimmy Allen*. One of the first mystery men to take to the airwaves was the Lone Ranger. Originating at the studios of WXYZ in Detroit, the adventures of the masked rider of the plains were aired after the children's hour, in complete half-hour episodes three times a week. The show was first broadcast in January of 1933 and eventually was heard on stations throughout the country. It was sponsored regionally, by an assortment of bread companies.

WXYZ did so well with their first masked man that they introduced another one in 1936, a contemporary urban avenger known as the Green Hornet. With his mask, gas gun, powerful automobile, faithful chauffeur, and vigilante ways, the Hornet was to prove an important influence on later creators of comic book heroes.

An equally inspiring figure of radio mystery was the Shadow, heard once a week in a half-hour format, commencing in 1937. Portrayed originally by twenty-two- year-old Orson Welles, the radio Shadow differed from his pulp counterpart. His civilian identity was definitely that of wealthy man about town Lamont Cranston, his friend and companion was the lovely Margo Lane and, a definite plus, he had the ability to become invisible. Less a coldblooded avenger than his pulp counterpart, the radio Shadow dealt not only with crooks and criminal masterminds but with madmen, monsters, and an entertaining variety of occult terrors. Though he also appealed to an adult listening audience, the Shadow had a large youth following and was obviously highly thought of by several of the artists and writers who were earning their living in comic books.

Of the other popular kid radio shows of the 1930s, some were adapted from the funny papers and some were created expressly for radio. All told, the kid shows comprised a large list that included *Jack Armstrong*, *Tom Mix*, *Dick Tracy*, *Tarzan*, *Buck Rogers*, *Chandu the Magician*, *Smilin' Jack*, *Terry and the Pirates*, and *Captain Midnight*. Wheaties, Ovaltine, and Hot Ralston were typical of the sponsoring products.

By the late 1930s, popular media in America encompassed film, radio, and pulp magazines. The modern-format comic book had been established and the number of regularly issued titles was increasing. Although most editors, writers, and artists were freely assimilating types of characters and storytelling methods of newspaper funnies and other media, some of them were beginning to realize that the comic book was a separate medium altogether. It was a canny observation, but what was needed now to turn the blossoming business into a full-scale industry was the right kind of hero.

Captain Midnight, another great aviator, starred in a popular radio show for children and, here, his own Big Little Book.

©1937 by General Mills, Inc.

CHAPTER 5

It's...Superman!

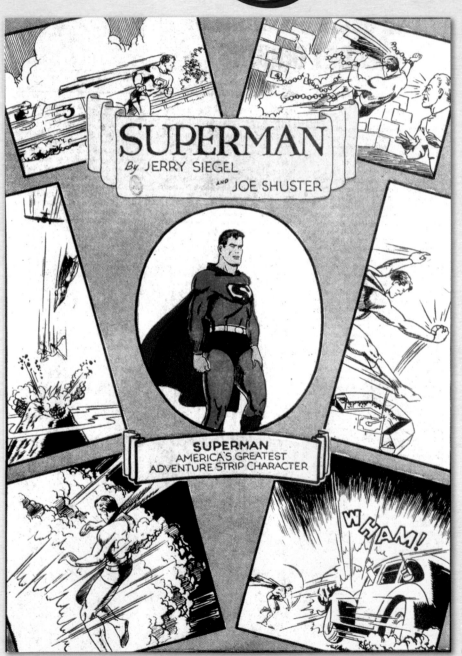

SUPERMAN
by JERRY SIEGEL
AND JOE SHUSTER

SUPERMAN
AMERICA'S GREATEST
ADVENTURE STRIP CHARACTER

WHAM!

*C*omic books needed help—it was definitely a job for Superman. The trouble was that no comic book publisher seemed to realize that the Man of Steel was exactly the sort of hero that was needed to revolutionize the business. The creation of a pair of teenagers—writer Jerry Siegel and artist Joe Shuster—Superman was born in Cleveland, Ohio in the early 1930s. He languished there for several years, making occasional assaults on Manhattan and trying to get somebody to pay attention to him. Finally, in 1938, the big guy got a break and started appearing in *Action Comics*. Single-handedly he (and alter-ego Clark Kent) turned comic books into big business, changing their look and content forever. He also made several of the people associated with him impressively rich. For a while, even his creators prospered. The notion of a superman was, obviously, not a new one; tales of super men date back to antiquity. Siegel and Shuster certainly drew from classical influences, but also took cues from Philip Wylie's 1930 novel *Gladiator*, which had introduced a contemporary version of the superman concept. The book's hero, Hugo Danner, possesses exceptional physical strength and is very nearly invulnerable. According to Wylie's biographer, Truman Frederick Keefer, "One of the main challenges to Wylie in writing *Gladiator*

Jerry Siegel and Joe Shuster's Superman is one of the greatest fictional characters of all time. His 1938 debut made a splash big enough to establish comics as a major force in American publishing. The early Superman illustration seen here was not published until the 1980s. Joe Shuster's layout has additional art by Paul Cassidy, John Sikela, Eddie Dobrotka, and Lee Nowak.

©1990 by DC Comics, Inc.

was the need to devise spectacular feats for Hugo to perform and then to make them seem probable. Our exposure to the *Superman* comic strip unfortunately obscures the originality of many of these inventions, which, according to Wylie, as well as recent scholars, were 'borrowed' from *Gladiator*. Hugo hurtling across a river in a single leap, bounding fifty feet straight up in the air, holding a cannon above his head with one arm, killing a shark by ripping its jaws apart, felling a charging bull with a fist between the eyes, lifting an automobile by its bumper and turning it around in the road—all of these were, in 1930, fresh and new and very exciting to read about."

Superman was influenced by other fictional heroes, as well. There were earlier dual-identity heroes like Zorro and the Shadow, and there was Doc Savage, whose first name was Clark. Siegel told the *Saturday Evening Post* that he'd conceived the character this way— "I am lying in bed counting sheep when all of a sudden it hits me. I

conceive a character like Samson, Hercules and all the strong men I ever heard of rolled into one. Only more so."

Siegel was also aware of the tremendous appeal of his basic concept. "You see, Clark Kent grew not only out of my private life, but also out of Joe's," Siegel told an interviewer a few years ago. "As a high school student, I thought that some day I might become a reporter, and I had crushes on several attractive girls who either didn't know I existed or didn't care I existed. It occurred to me: What if I was real terrific? What if I had something special going for me, like jumping over buildings or throwing cars around or something like that? Then maybe they would notice me."

Indeed, it is the mild-mannered Clark Kent who gives Superman such great and enduring appeal. Worthy but underappreciated, Kent is the alter-ego not just of Superman, but of many of Superman's fans. Siegel nailed it when he remembered that he had wanted to be noticed. Superman provided Clark with a way to be noticed, and provided the same thing, vicariously, to the comic's readers.

Initially, it was syndicates and comic book editors who failed to notice *Superman*. A typical rejection letter for the strip read, "We are in the market only for strips likely to have the most extraordinary appeal, and we do not feel

Above: Rescuing beautiful women who had fallen out of windows became a familiar part of Superman's routine.

©1940 by DC Comics, Inc.

Right: Superman proved himself as useful under the sea as on land and in the air.

©1939 by DC Comics, Inc.

This page from *Superman* #1 originally appeared in the first issue of *Action Comics*—where Superman made his official debut. Note that Superman's flying was initially more like leaping and his familiar "S" crest was not yet finalized.

©1939 by DC Comics, Inc.

that *Superman* gets into that category." Sheldon Mayer was a bit more astute. "What happened was this," he once explained. "It came into the McClure Syndicate, offered as a strip. I went nuts over the thing; it was the thing we were all looking for. It struck me as having the elements that were popular in the movies, all the elements that were popular in novels, and all the elements that I loved."

The problem was Mayer couldn't convince M. C. Gaines or any of the McClure officials to sign on the feature. "They asked me what I thought of it. I thought it was great. And they kept sending it back." Mayer's persistence got Gaines interested enough to look the material over again. "He took it and looked at it and read it, and he said, 'You think this is good?' And I said, Yeah!'"

Rather than persuade the syndicate to use *Superman*, Gaines "had a better idea. He was going to take it up and offer it as a comic book so we could get the printing out of it. In other words, he was a proper businessman. He knew where he stood."

Just before his departure from the company, Major Nicholson had worked with his staff on a fourth title. It was to be called either *Action Funnies* or *Action Comics*. The major didn't get to see that one through and by the time DC's *Action Comics* was ready to roll, he was out on the street. Legend has it that Gaines showed the *Superman* strips to Harry Donenfeld himself and persuaded the publisher to add the feature to the forthcoming magazine. Vincent Sullivan, who was editor of *Action*, recalled things somewhat differently. "Donenfeld had little or nothing to do with the selection of features and things of that nature," he once explained. The samples were shown directly to editor Sullivan. "When they showed this thing to me that they'd been trying to sell, it looked good to me, and I started it. That's how *Superman* got going."

The story that appeared in *Action Comics* #1 (June 1938) offered a one-page introduction to the new hero, listing his birthplace only as "a distant planet" and making no mention of his real or adoptive parents. Page two began in the middle of the story, with *Superman* carrying a pretty nightclub singer through the air. The story ends with the words "to be continued." Siegel and Shuster's final panel said, "And so begins the startling adventures of the most sensational strip character of all time: SUPERMAN!" The grammar may have been weak, but the predictive aspect was dead on.

That first adventure was, according to Shuster, "taken directly from the newspaper strip. They were in a rush to meet the deadline on the first issue. Everything happened very fast. They made the decision to publish it and said to us, 'Just get out and turn out 13 pages based on your strip.' It was a rush job. The only solution Jerry and I could come up with was to cut up the strips into panels and paste the panels on a sheet the size of the page."

The first *Action* cover was adapted from a panel in the story. "When Harry Donenfeld first saw that cover of Superman holding that car in the air," Mayer recalled, "he really got worried. He felt that nobody would believe it, that

it was ridiculous . . . crazy." Possibly because of that, the next few covers didn't show Superman or even mention him. Drawn by Leo O'Mealia, they showed scenes of plausible adventure involving airplanes, Arabs, and Mounties. At the time, no one except Siegel, Shuster, and Mayer had great expectations for *Superman*. Vince Sullivan, when asked if he'd anticipated the new hero's success, replied, "No, I don't think anybody did." He said he'd simply bought the feature because "it looked good. It was different and there was a lot of action. This is what kids wanted."

The public, heavily weighted with Depression-reared kids who wanted the most they could get for their dimes, was far quicker than DC to grasp the new character's appeal. From the moment the youngsters saw Superman lift that car over his head, they recognized that he was something special. But according to John Kobler's profile of Siegel and Shuster in the June 21, 1941 issue of the *Saturday Evening Post*, the sales on the first three issues

of *Action* were not particularly impressive. "But with the fourth, *Action Comics* spurted mysteriously ahead of its fellow publications," Kobler related. "Donenfeld heard the rumble of distant drums. 'We better have a newsstand

Beautiful in its elegance and simplicity, the cover of *Superman* #1 epitomizes the character's timeless appeal.

©1939 by DC Comics, Inc.

survey,' said he. The survey quickened his brightened hopes. Children were clamoring not for *Action Comics*, but for 'that magazine with Superman on it.' Quivering with excitement, Donenfeld ordered Superman splashed all over the cover of succeeding issues. They sold out."

The sales of *Action* quickly rose to 500,000 a month and by 1941 the magazine was selling 900,000 copies of each issue. The *Superman* magazine, started in 1939, soon reached a circulation of 1,250,000 and grossed $950,000 in 1940.

Superman continued to proliferate. He got a newspaper strip of his own, syndicated by McClure. It was here, in this newspaper strip, that a detailed account of the destruction of the planet Krypton was given for the first time, along with scenes of the baby Superman being rocketed to Earth, like a streamlined Moses, in a ship of his father's invention. The strip devoted two whole weeks to Superman's parents, Jor-L and Lora, and to all the dire seismic events leading up to his emigration. By the third week Superman, in his guise of Clark Kent, was seen working as a mild-mannered reporter and had met co-worker Lois Lane.

Some of the best-known dramatic lines associated with the character originated not in the comics but on the radio show. This program, inaugurated on a national basis early in 1940, was heard mostly in the eastern United States during its first few months. Eventually, three fifteen-minute episodes were broadcast each week from New York, airing in most parts of the nation on Monday, Wednesday, and Friday sometime between five and six in the evening. Clayton "Bud" Collyer starred; the adventures were narrated by Jackson Beck.

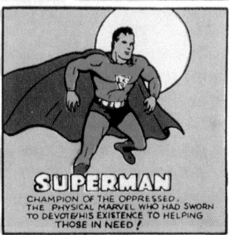

Superman was not merely the "champion of the oppressed"—he was a bona fide publishing phenomenon.

©1990 by DC Comics, Inc.

It was the radio show that introduced such memorable phrases as, "Up, up and away!" and "This is a job for . . . Superman!" The show's opening was built around two other unforgettable bits of copy. "Faster than a speeding bullet, more powerful than a locomotive, able to leap tall buildings at a single bound. . . ." is one of them. This was chiefly a variation on introductory copy Siegel had written for the first issues of *Action* and *Superman*. The speeding bullet doesn't appear there, though, and the locomotive was called a "streamline train." The radio program's extolling of Superman's abilities was followed by, "Look! Up in the sky! It's a bird! It's a plane! It's . . . Superman!" If there is an art to the

writing of radio copy, it reached its zenith here.

In order to meet the increasing demand for Superman comic book stories and maintain *Slam Bradley*, *Federal Men*, *Spy*, and their other features, Siegel and Shuster had to hire additional artists. In 1938 ads began running in artists' and writers' magazines: "Help wanted. Artist with ability to draw action-adventure strips; assist on nationally established features. Send samples. Joseph E. Shuster, 10905 Amor Ave., Cleveland, Ohio."

Wayne Boring, who'd worked as a salesman of advertising art and put in a stint assisting on the *Big Chief Wahoo* comic strip, responded to the ad with samples. Shortly thereafter, he found himself working in Cleveland in a shop with other new recruits, Paul Cassidy and Leo Nowak. "We had an office 12 by 12 with four drawing boards set up there," Boring recalled. "Jerry had a desk in the anteroom . . . it was the smallest office in Cleveland. At first Joe would sketch out pretty lightly, and we'd work over it."

Later, as Shuster's eyesight worsened, the assistants did more and more of the work. Siegel and Shuster's dreams

about *Superman* were now coming true. But they were finding that creating a character that earns millions of dollars doesn't always mean you'll make millions yourself. When DC bought *Superman*, Jack Liebowitz had explained to the pair that they had to sign a release giving all rights to the feature to the publisher. "It is customary for all our contributors to release all rights to us," he wrote. "This is the businesslike way of doing things." Liebowtiz wasn't trying to con the boys—this was indeed the common practice throughout the comic book field and the situation didn't change at all until fairly recently. The partners were paid $130 for that first *Superman* job—ten dollars a page. That meant, as journalist John Kobler pointed out back in 1941, they would "be relinquishing their equity in all possible future profits from syndication, radio, movies, and so on, and that Harry Donenfeld, as sole owner of *Superman*, could even hire some other team to draw him." Conflict loomed.

As their character's popularity increased, Siegel started asking for more money. At first Liebowitz contended that the success of *Action Comics* was only partially due to the Man of Steel. When it became impossible to deny the impact *Superman* was having, the situation changed. "It was only after anguished appeals that Siegel and Shuster finally managed, in 1940, to wangle sizable profits for themselves,"

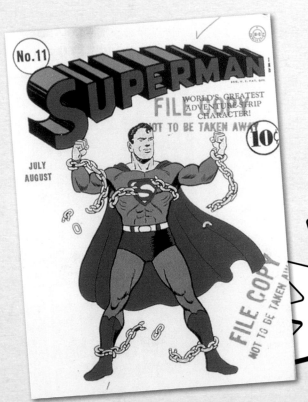

The stocky and muscular Superman of the early 1940s was a hero for the common man.

©1941 by DC Comics, Inc.

Superman was equally willing to deal with the pettiest thugs and most powerful criminal masterminds, making him a democratic sort of crimefighter.

©1941 by DC Comics, Inc.

reported the Post article. "$75,000, of which $16,000 goes in staff salaries and overhead. . . . Their syndicate profits have leaped to $600 a week. . . . Next year, with their revenues from radio, movies, and licenses coming in, they stand to make $150,000. Their ten-year term of service, however, is not reciprocal. Donenfeld remains free at any time to discharge them."

The importance of *Superman* was noticed by the business community fairly quickly. As early as 1942, *Business Week* reported that comics had become big time and that kids were spending an estimated fifteen million dollars a year on them. The weekly stated, "Superman has shown the way in a new field of publishing."

For the rest of the year following the advent of the Man of Steel, though, no further superheroes were introduced, not even by DC. And only two new costumed crimefighters, neither of whom had a single super power, entered comics.

The earliest costumed hero to venture onto the newsstands in the wake of *Superman* was not especially impressive. He possessed no special powers and wore a baggy costume that resembled a hooded business suit. Fighting crime with a bow and arrow, he called himself the Arrow and could be found in *Funny Pages* from #21 (September 1938) onward. Paul Gustavson was the artist and writer. The Arrow was one of those mysterious fellows who just seemed to know when a crime was taking place. If a lovely blonde heiress was about to be attacked in a mansion at midnight by a "huge, grotesque figure," the Arrow would suddenly leap into the room and his bowstring would start twanging. Should a handsome couple be stranded in a mad doctor's mysterious house "high in the Rocky Mountains, miles away from civilization," you could be certain the Arrow would save the day with a well-placed shaft.

The Crimson Avenger, whom we met previously, was the only other dress-up crimebuster to come forward in 1938. He commenced wielding his gas gun in *Detective Comics* a month after the Arrow first dipped into his quiver.

The first authentic *superhero* to set up shop in competition with Superman was created by the unlikely team of

Victor S. Fox and Will Eisner, and first appeared in the spring of 1939. The British-born Fox had spent twenty years on Wall Street and left it, with a less than spotless reputation, to go to work as an accountant for Detective Comics, Inc. at 480 Lexington Avenue in Manhattan. While contemplating the increasingly impressive sales figures of *Action Comics*, he decided to start his own funny book company. After moving to gloomy offices on another floor of the same building that housed DC, Fox got in touch with the Eisner-Iger

shop. Jerry Iger handled the business details, Will Eisner handled the creative end. "We were," Eisner has said, "delivering instant comic books to publishers."

According to Eisner, Fox had in mind a comic book that would star a character to be called Wonder Man. This new hero was to have a red costume, but the rest of the specifications "were almost identical to Superman," Eisner has said. "We knew it was very much like Superman, that it was imitative, but we had no idea of its legal implications."

Eisner wrote and drew Wonder Man's first and, as it turned out, only adventure and signed it with the name Willis. Unlike Superman, Wonder Man was blond and he was not an extraterrestrial. He picked up his many impressive abilities— which included leaping over tall buildings in a single bound, catching explosive shells in his bare hands, smashing through solid walls, and so forth—in Tibet, the magical-powers capital of the world. An ancient mystic trained him and gave him a special ring "as a symbol of the Herculean powers with which you are endowed. As long as you wear it you will be the strongest human on Earth and will be impervious."

In everyday life Wonder Man was Fred Carson, "a timid radio engineer and inventor." The fourteen-page story in *Wonder Comics* #1 (May 1939)

found Fred journeying, along with the debutante daughter of his boss at the IBC network, to a mythical European country to cover a war. Before too long he "removes his outer garments and becomes Wonder Man, mightiest human on Earth." Subsequently he behaves in a Superman-like manner.

Or so Harry Donenfeld, the head man at DC, contended. "[Donenfeld] hit Fox real hard," Eisner has recalled, "and right away." Detective Comics, Inc. 85 sued Fox for infringement of copyright. ▶

Siegel & Shuster

Jerry Siegel (left) and Joe Shuster appear with Superman in this 1942 caricature.

©1990 by DC Comics, Inc.

   Writer Jerry Siegel and artist Joe Shuster met while attending Cleveland's Glenville High School. The pair always knew that their creation, Superman, was destined for great things. Long before they'd received so much as a friendly nibble from a publisher or syndicate editor, they were working on merchandising details. "One day I read an article in some leading magazine about how Tarzan was merchandised by Stephen Slesinger so successfully," Siegel once recalled. "And I thought: Wow! Superman is even more super than Tarzan. The same [merchandising] could happen with Superman. And I mentioned it to Joe. He got real enthusiastic, and I walked in a day or so later, and he had made a big drawing of Superman, showing how the character could be merchandised on boxtops, T-shirts, and everything." Shuster added, "In this drawing we just let our imagination run wild. We visualized Superman toys, games and a radio show—that was before TV—and Superman movies. We even visualized Superman billboards. And it's all come true."

   Both the partners were avid movie and pulp magazine buffs, and shared an abiding interest in science fiction. In 1932, they began to collaborate on a mimeographed fanzine, entitled simply *Science Fiction*, that mixed articles and fiction. The January 1933 issue of the shortlived effort contained a story, written by Siegel and illustrated by Shuster, called "The Reign of the Superman." In it, the superman of the title was a villain.

   "A couple of months after I published this story," Siegel has said, "it occurred to me that a superman as a hero rather than a villain might make a great comic strip character in the vein of Tarzan, only more super and sensational than that great character. Joe and I drew it up as a comic book—this was early in 1933. We interested a publisher in putting it out, but then he changed his mind, and that was the end of that particular version of Superman." In this early incarnation, Superman had super powers but no costume—"he was simply wearing a T-shirt and pants."

Eventually, of course, Superman found a home and became a publishing phenomenon. As the years passed and the team's creation piled up profits, Siegel and Shuster grew increasingly unhappy. In 1947, when their joint annual income had dropped to $46,000, they decided to go to court. The April 14, 1947 issue of *Newsweek* reported, "In the New York Supreme Court in Westchester County [Siegel and Shuster] had filed suit seeking (1) to regain the rights to their brainchild, (2) to cancel their newspaper syndication contract with McClure and their contract with [publisher Harry] Donenfeld on the ground that they have been violated, and (3) to recover about $5,000,000 they say Superman should have brought them over a nine-year period."

Newsweek went on to note a conflict over the Superboy character. "When Siegel was in the army, Superboy made his debut under the double byline. Siegel claimed he never authorized such use of his name and has never received a cent for the strip."

Siegel and Shuster did not fare well. While the court eventually ruled that "Detective Comics, Inc. acted illegally" as far as Superboy was concerned, DC did indeed own Superman. The partners were paid for Superboy, in a settlement rumored to be around $50,000 to each, but they were fired by Donenfeld. Siegel and Shuster had been separated from their creation.

The team turned their attention to other projects. *Funnyman*, which was both a newspaper strip and a comic book in the late 1940s (the latter published by their old Action editor, Vincent Sullivan), did not succeed. The pair devoted nearly the next three decades to various legal actions intended to help them regain ownership of Superman. It wasn't until 1975, with the first of the multimillion-dollar Superman movies in the preproduction phase, that DC, by then owned by Warner Communications, agreed on a financial settlement with the creators. In recent years Siegel and Shuster have had what's been reported as "a good relationship with DC."

The first adventure of Superboy appeared in *More Fun Comics* #101 in 1944. Siegel and Shuster had to go to court in order to be compensated by DC for use of the character.

©1944 by DC Comics, Inc.

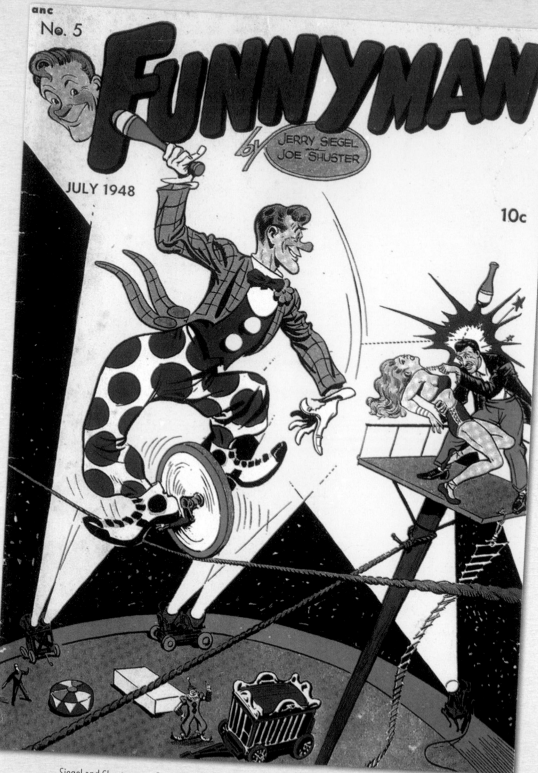

anc
No. 5

FUNNYMAN

by JERRY SIEGEL JOE SHUSTER

JULY 1948

10c

Siegel and Shuster were fired by DC after asking for fair compensation as the creators of Superman. *Funnyman*, the team's 1947 attempt to duplicate the success of Superman, failed after just six issues.

©1948 by Magazine Enterprises, Inc.

The case reached the federal district court for New York City, in 1940. At that time the judge ruled in favor of DC. But Wonder Man was a long time dead by then, since Fox never risked the character's second appearance. But the enterprising Fox, whom Eisner remembers as having the manner and morals of the sort of movie gangster portrayed by Edward G. Robinson, didn't give up his dream of cashing in on what he was certain would be a superhero boom. Victor Fox would return.

Detective Comics #27 appeared at just about the same time as the first issue of *Wonder* and contained DC's next entry in the superhero derby. There on the cover was a costumed fellow called The Batman, swinging over the rooftops with an armlock around the throat of a hoodlum in a green pinstripe suit. Inside, the new hero led off the issue in a short, six-page story. Although the pointy ears on his cowl were a little lopsided, and his batwing cape didn't fit exactly right, there was something intriguing about him.

Batman typified the ability of the original-material comic books to deliver pulp magazine and movie elements in a funny paper format. The popular entertainments the artists and writers of this growing new industry had enjoyed as children were now recycled and turned into comic book stories. Batman is one of the most successful examples of this, inspired by movie melodramas and pulpwood yarns but becoming a distinctive character in his own right.

Bill Finger, the original writer of the feature, once said, "My first script was a take-off on a *Shadow* story . . . I patterned my style of writing *Batman* after the *Shadow*. Also after Warner Bros. movies, the gangster movies." Bob Kane, Batman's original artist, has mentioned that another source of inspiration was a 1926 movie called *The Bat*, "in which the villain wore a batlike costume which was quite awesome."

In its earliest incarnation, *The Bat* was a highly popular Broadway play by Avery Hopwood and Mary Roberts Rinehart. It was filmed for the first time in 1926 and again in 1931 under the title *The Bat Whispers*, with tough guy Chester Morris taking top billing. Basically an "old dark house" story, it had to do with stolen money, secret rooms and hidden passages, and a crazed killer who dresses up like a bat. The nightstalking Bat of the 1931 version certainly seems to be an ancestor of Batman, particularly when prowling the rooftops and casting his weird shadow across walls. Kane is on record as having been influenced by this movie.

In civilian life Batman was Bruce Wayne, "a bored young socialite." When night fell, however, playboy Wayne became "powerful and awesome," a "weird menace to all crime." Unlike his more sedate contemporaries in the private investigator line, Batman didn't wait for cases to come to him. He ▶

Bob Kane & Bill Finger

Bob Kane is the acknowledged creator of Batman.

©Wide World Photos

Batman was the creation of a young man from the Bronx who'd drawn gag cartoons and humorous fillers before trying his hand at more serious fare. He had considerable help from a young shoe salesman who aspired to be a writer. Eventually, the production of the adventures of their increasingly popular hero would require a whole crew of artists, writers, and editors.

For artist Bob Kane, Batman has meant more than five decades of public recogniton and accolade. Kane began his professional career in 1936, drawing *Hiram Hick*, a funny feature that appeared in Henle Publishing's short-lived *Wow Comics*. The editor there was Jerry Iger and when Iger and Will Eisner formed a shop in the following year, the twenty-one year old Kane was invited to join the staff. He drew *Jest Laffs* and other gag cartoons, and a comedy-adventure strip titled *Peter Pupp*. These ran in Fiction House's *Jumbo Comics*. The Pupp feature, which was probably at least partly inspired by Floyd Gottfredson's *Mickey Mouse* newspaper strip, allowed Kane to deal for the first time with some of the elements he'd later treat more seriously in *Batman*. Pete was a daring little fellow; a typical four-page sequence sent him up in a fighter plane to combat a giant robot. The robot was controlled by a satanic villain whose forehead was adorned with a single eye.

Kane's first sales to DC were also in the humor line—one- and two-page comedy fillers. These were *Professor Doolittle*, a pantomime effort for *Adventure Comics*; *Ginger Snap*, about a wise little girl, for *More Fun; and Oscar the Gumshoe* for *Detective*.

In the Bob Kane entry in Jerry Bails's *Who's Who of American Comics*, Kane lists the artists who were major influences on him: Alex Raymond, Billy DeBeck, and Milton Caniff. Kane's first serious feature, *Rusty and His Pals*, shows the Caniff influence clearly. *Rusty* started in *Adventure* in 1938 and dealt with three boys and their Pat Ryan-type mentor, Steve Carter. Like Terry of Caniff's *Terry and the Pirates*, Rusty and company tangled with pirates and sinister Orientals. Kane's drawing on the early episodes was cartoony, but picked up a more serious look as *Rusty* progressed, even emulating Caniff's bold style of inking.

The scripts for Kane's first attempt at adventure were provided by his Bronx neighbor, Bill Finger. Two years older than Kane and working at selling shoes, Finger was a dedicated movie fan and reader of the pulps. The two met at a party and later decided to collaborate.

Kane and Finger followed *Rusty and His Pals* with *Batman*. Next came *Clip Carson*, which began in *Action Comics* #14 (July 1939). "I've always liked Rider Haggard's *King Solomon's Mines*," Finger once explained. "So I thought we might have a great white hunter type—one whose adventures would take him anywhere, Africa, South America, anywhere."

Finger never received a byline on any of the Kane features. It wasn't until he helped create the Green Lantern for DC in 1940 that his name began to appear in comic books. Except for a period in which he wrote for television, Bill Finger remained in comics for most of his life. He died in 1974.

This simple but dynamic page is from *Detective Coics* #27—the comic book that introduced Batman to the world. Writer Bill Finger and artist Bob Kane created a great fictional hero who endures today.

©1939 by DC Comics, Inc.

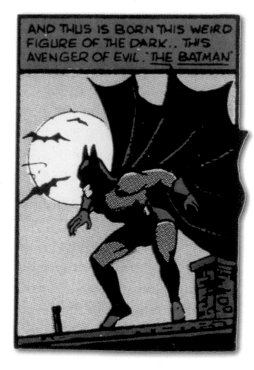

Batman's origin was revealed in *Detective Comics* #33.

prowled the city—New York in the earliest adventures and later Gotham City—looking for trouble. He always found it, dropping down to shock the bejeesus out of burglars, kidnappers, and murderers. Although not above wisecracking while tangling with groups of a half dozen or more gunmen, Batman was a pretty grim vigilante in his early days. Besides his gadget-laden utility belt, he carried a .45 automatic and wasn't reluctant to use it. A trained athlete and acrobat, he was capable of breaking a man's neck with a well-placed kick.

Batman's origin, the inside story of "who he is and how he came to be," didn't appear until *Detective* #33 (November 1939). In a terse two-page account readers were told that fifteen years earlier Bruce Wayne's parents were gunned down on the street by a stickup man. The boy, a witness to the crime, vowed to dedicate his life to "warring on criminals." Having no supernatural powers, Wayne had to work at becoming a hero. He devoted years to preparing for his crimefighting career, turning himself into both a master scientist and crackerjack athlete. Deciding that he'd need a disguise capable of striking terror into the hearts of criminals, he was inspired by the intrusion of a bat into his den. "It's an omen . . . I shall become a BAT!"

Another major event in Batman's life was recounted in *Detective* #38 (April 1940): He acquired a sidekick. "An exciting new figure whose incredible gymnastic and athletic feats will astound you," a blurb proclaimed. "A laughing, fighting young daredevil who scoffs at danger like the legendary Robin Hood whose name and spirit he has adopted . . . Robin the Boy Wonder." Bob Kane once explained, "In my subconscious mind I longed to be like Robin when I was his age, fighting alongside his idol Batman (or, in my case, Doug Fairbanks, Sr.). I figured Robin would appeal to all children of his age group as an identifiable person for their inner fantasies."

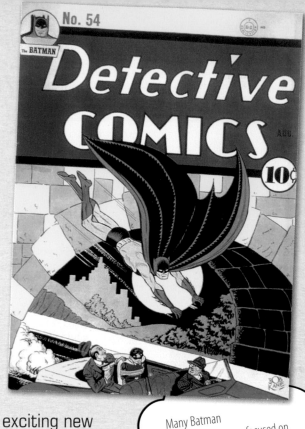

Many Batman covers over the years focused on the hero's acrobatic skills. This 1941 cover was probably drawn by Jerry Robinson.

Bill Finger amplified, "Batman was a combination of Fairbanks and Sherlock Holmes. Holmes had his Watson. The thing that bothered me was that Batman didn't have anyone to talk to, and it got a little tiresome always having him thinking. I found as I went along that Batman needed a Watson to talk to. That's how Robin came to be. Bob called me over and said he was going to put a boy in the story to identify with Batman. I thought it was a great idea."

Jerry Robinson, Kane's assistant at the time, had a few more facts to add about the dynamic youth's gestation. "I thought of Batman's new partner as a sort of young Robin Hood... I remember plugging the name Robin against the others that didn't seem quite as good," he recalled. "Once we agreed on the name, I suggested adapting Robin Hood's costume for the new character."

Why exactly did Batman and Robin succeed where so many other superheroes failed? For one thing, there was the look of Bob Kane's art work. His primitive, cartoony style, carried on and polished by Robinson, fit the sort of melodramatic, nighttime stories he and Finger loved to spin. "Batman's world took control of the reader," Jules Feiffer has observed. "Kane's was an authentic fantasy, a genuine vision, so that, however one might nitpick the components, the end product remained an impregnable whole: gripping and original." The stories, particularly in the World War II years, were good, borrowing from writers O. Henry and Damon Runyon, and from the movies. And, of course, Batman and Robin battled some of the all-time best villains in comics—bizarre figures like the Joker, the Penguin, the Riddler, and Catwoman.

In the summer of 1939 the

Artist Charles Wojtkowski adopted the pen name Charles Nicholas when drawing the adventures of the Blue Beetle. This panel is from a 1939 issue of *Mystery Men Comics*.

unconquerable Victor Fox came back into the fray. He introduced not one but three new costumed heroes. The third issue of *Wonderworld* (July 1939), which is what Fox was now calling *Wonder*, introduced the Flame, another product of the Eisner-Iger packaging establishment. The initial adventures of the yellow-clad superman were handsomely rendered by Lou Fine, a fine draftsman with a gift for classically heroic figure work. A slow starter, the Flame took several issues to really ignite. When he first showed up, he didn't appear to have any superpowers at all. Confused racketeers asked him questions like, "Who are you? What do you want?" In subsequent issues he displayed an ability to materialize out of smoke and flame. A while later he really started living up to

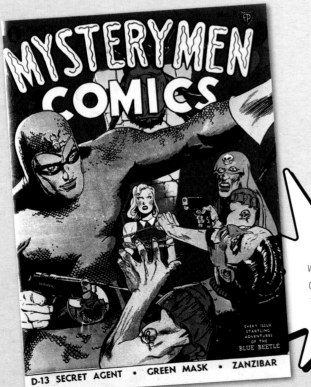

This *Mystery Men* cover was drawn by Lou Fine, one of the best artists of the "Golden Age" of comics.

Lou Fine illustrated the adventures of the Flame for publisher Victor Fox.

©1940 by Fox Features Syndicate

fast cars, sinister Orientals, snarling gangsters, big city backgrounds. "The Green Mask wasn't much of a mystery man," comics historian Robert Jennings has observed, "since he had no secret identity, no background, and no unusual powers. He did wear a pretty bizarre costume, but he relied more on a blazing automatic pistol than super strength to solve his problems."

Several issues, and artists, later the Mask did acquire a few more of the accouterments of his trade. A caption informed readers, "Michael Selby, placed in a vita-ray machine, discovers that the supercharged shocks have made him a miracle man. He can zoom through the air and perform super-human feats." The Mask also picked up a boy companion named Domino. Although never a particularly engaging character, The Mask did look appropriately heroic on early covers by Lou Fine.

Soon, however, the Mask lost his star slot to the book's other resident superhero, the Blue Beetle. This unusually named character started out near the back of the book,

biding his time in short four-page adventures. Until his second appearance, he didn't even have a crimefighting costume. Eventually he started showing up for work in the distinctive blue, chain mail outfit and black domino mask that became his trademark. Wisely, he abandoned the bug antennae he'd briefly worn on his cowl.

The Blue Beetle's early escapades were drawn by Charles Wojtkowski, who'd adopted the pen name Charles Nicholas. The Beetle was one of the few superheroes who acquired his powers through attention to his diet—captions continually reminded readers that he was "given super-energy by vitamin 2X." His chain mail outfit, by the way, made

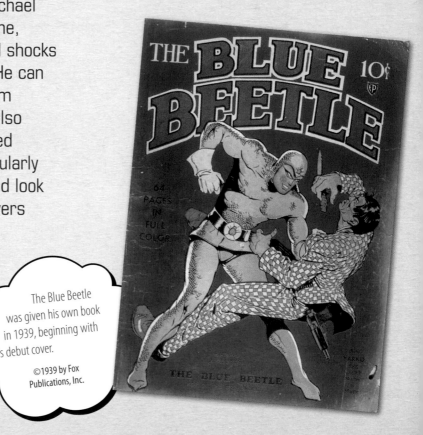

The Blue Beetle was given his own book in 1939, beginning with this debut cover.

©1939 by Fox Publications, Inc.

his name, revealing a hitherto unsuspected knack for bursting into flame, burning through walls, and performing similarly fiery stunts. In *Wonderworld* #30 (October 1941) the Flame acquired a female companion. Known as Flame Girl, she stuck with him until the magazine died only three issues later.

Fox's second magazine was *Mystery Men Comics* and in this one he offered two costumed heroes. The intended leading man was the Green Mask, who wore a blue costume and cape and a green headrag mask. The artist was Walter Frehm, who'd been Will Gould's assistant on *Red Barry*. The Green Mask feature had the same cartoony-adventure look of that cops and robbers newspaper strip—blazing automatics, him "almost invulnerable." Once powered by 2X, the Blue Beetle would run around for eight or ten pages, cracking skulls and making wisecracks, while he hunted down a crazed scientist called Doc and other, peculiarly named villains: the Wart, Scrag, the Eel, and Mr. Downhill.

The Blue Beetle became Fox's most popular character. He moved to the front of *Mystery Men* and was showcased on every cover beginning with issue #7 (February 1940). He got a magazine all his own before a year was out and for awhile appeared in a newspaper strip drawn by Jack Kirby. Victor Fox even managed to promote a Blue Beetle radio show starring character actor Frank Lovejoy—"Thrilling Drama of the Avenging Gang Smasher . . . Twice-a-Week."

Centaur Publications' Amazing Man, an early creation of artist Bill Everett, first appeared in the fall of 1939. *Amazing Man Comics* skipped the first four issues and commenced with #5. The character's origin came about this way—"25 years ago, in the mountains of Tibet, the Council of Seven selected an orphan of superb physical structure, and each did his part to develop in the child all the qualities of one who would dominate the world of men with his great strength, knowledge and courage . . . His friend Nika, the young chemist, endowed him with the power to make himself disappear in a cloud of green

vapor, and extracted from him the promise to always be good and kind and generous."

Before graduating and being sent to America to combat evil, A-Man had to undergo a series of tests that made your average college midterm or IRS tax audit look like a cinch. Among the hurdles he overcame were a tug-of-war match with a bull elephant and a tussle with a cobra —while his hands were tied behind his back. The main snag to an uncomplicated career of crime-stopping was a rogue member of the Council of Seven itself. A sinister hooded figure with the power of telepathy, this villain, the Great Question, "covets plans of dire evil for the boy." Needless to say, Amazing Man had his work cut out for him.

Timely (later Marvel) Comics came up with *Marvel Comics* (*Marvel Mystery Comics* as of issue #2), which went on sale late in 1939. This title offered a pair of superheroes who would enjoy long popularity, the Human Torch and the Sub- Mariner. The Human Torch, who grabbed the cover of the premiere issue, wasn't actually human. Rather, he was a "synthetic man—an exact replica of a human being." His origin story is not exactly coherent, but it seems that one Professor Horton, who had been work- ing to create a synthetic human, holds a press conference to announce that, although he's succeeded, he has some doubts. "I call him THE HUMAN TORCH,"

Marvel Mystery became synonymous with nonstop action. The comic's stars, Sub-Mariner and the Human Torch, stood out among the comic book heroes of the 1940s.

©1941 by Timely Comics, Inc.

Horton explains as he unveils a large airtight glass cylinder that contains his blond, red-suited creation. "Something went wrong with my figuring somewhere—every time the robot . . . contacts oxygen in the air, he bursts into flame!" Sure enough, as soon as Horton allows air into the cage, the Torch's figure is engulfed by fire. The gathered reporters, obviously lacking the true spirit of scientific inquiry, shout unhelpful things like, "Destroy that man!"

Although Horton does try to incapacitate his android by burying him in cement, that doesn't work and before

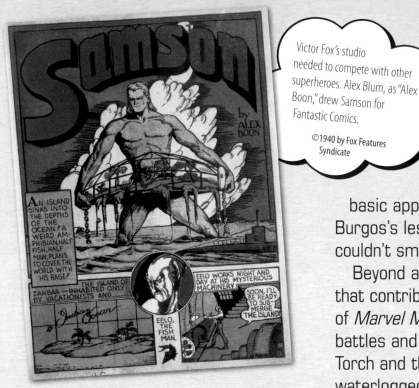

long "the HUMAN TORCH is on the loose again!" Appropriately enough, the Torch gets mixed up with arsonists and cleans up their dirty racket. By the end of the yarn he's learned to melt iron bars, throw fireballs, and turn his flame on and off at will. When the old professor suggests that the two of them might be able to make a fortune, the now-altruistic Torch informs his misguided creator, "No, Horton, I'll be free and no one will ever use me for selfish gain—or crime!"

What Carl Burgos, the artist-creator of the strip, had stumbled on was a basic idea that had tremendous appeal to kids. Most of us go through a phase in our youth where we're touched with a little pyromania—we play with matches,

we yearn for fireworks, we attempt to concoct fiery explosives with our chemistry sets. With the Human Torch readers had a hero who could play with fire and get away with it. The character's basic appeal was so strong that even Burgos's less-than-masterful drawing couldn't smother it.

Beyond a doubt, two of the things that contributed to the early success of *Marvel Mystery Comics* were the battles and subsequent team-ups of the Torch and the Sub-Mariner. Bill Everett's waterlogged Prince Namor, who'd first appeared in the extremely short-lived *Motion Picture Funnies Weekly*, had been raising hell from the very first issue of *Marvel*. Coming to Manhattan from his decimated undersea kingdom, Sub-Mariner was determined to get revenge. "You white devils have persecuted and tormented my people for years," he explains to policewoman Betty Dean, the pretty brunette with whom he carries on a love-hate relationship. Once in New York City, Namor behaves in the manner of an earlier and larger visitor named King Kong.

"He was an angry character," reflected Everett some years later. "He was probably expressing some of my own personality." With the angry Namor cutting up in the Big Apple and the

Human Torch freshly arrived to work as a cop, a confrontation was inevitable. "That was an idea Carl [Burgos] and I dreamed up," Everett once explained. "We considered the fact that the two characters and their opposing elements had separate stories and wondered what would happen if we got them together as rivals to fight each other." What happened was a battle royal that raged through Marvel #8 and #9 and wound up in a standoff in #10. But the next time these representatives of fire and water met, they were "fighting side by side!" As a caption in the 26-page team-up saga in *Marvel Mystery Comics* #17 (March 1941) explained, "The Human Torch and the Sub-Mariner are together again. Not to destroy each other but to form an alliance that will stop the gigantic plans for an invasion of the United States!"

Not to be outdone by Timely, Victor Fox was back yet again at the end of 1939 with another new magazine, *Fantastic Comics*, and another new superhero, Samson. This time the creative minds at the Eisner-Iger shop turned to the Bible for inspiration—"Out of the mist of history comes the mighty Samson. . . . Like his ancient forebears Samson pits his tremendous strength against the forces of evil and injustice." A "yellow-haired giant" whose costume consisted of thonged sandals and a pair of shaggy shorts, Samson's early adventures found him roughing up warmongers in mythical European countries. A humorless, dedicated chap who was driven by a compulsive need to "fight against crime and corruption," Samson favored a stunt in which he pulled down the pillars of a building and caused the walls to come tumbling down. Like his Biblical namesake, Samson's weak spot was his hair, and now and then he would be temporarily incapacitated when a giant robot or other rampaging bully tugged at his golden locks.

A year later, in the autumn of 1940, Samson followed the latest trend in comics by teaming up with blond lad named David. Since this feature was always of the no-frills sort, neither Samson nor his sidekick had a civilian identity. Most stories simply opened with them in shorts, ready to spring into action. A typical adventure gets rolling with the pair standing on a city street. "Samson! Look!" cries David, pointing upward. "A man falling from that building!" "Oh, Oh!" responds the yellow-haired giant. "I've got to work fast!" He picks up a nearby truck and holds it up over his head to catch the plummeting man. "Good thing this load of hay is handy!" And how. Alex Blum, a workhorse of the Eisner-Iger shop, was the first to draw mighty Samson's prosaic escapades; he was succeeded by Joe Simon, A1 Carreno, and others.

MLJ Magazines' The Wizard, who first appeared in *Top-Notch* #1 (December 1939), was much better dressed than Samson and probably smarter, too, for he was known as the Man With The Super Brain. Dapper as well as bright, the Wizard originally performed his deeds wearing black tie and tails, a cape, and a red domino mask. In that clean-shaven era, he was one of the few comic book heroes who wore a moustache. The Wiz's specialty was handling invasions and "plots against the government." In civilian life he was Blane Whitney, polo-playing scion of one of America's first families. "With his super-brain and photographic mind the Wizard is able to visualize far-away happenings. With these mental powers and his super-strength he ferrets out plots against the U.S."

In the Wizard's earliest battles, against such foreign scourges as the Jatsonian invaders and the equally nasty Borentals, he made use of many amazing weapons of his own invention. These included Secret Formula F 22 X, the H2-VX-O Ray, and his Dynamagno-Saw Ray Projector. Edd Ashe, Jr., was the first artist to bring all of this life; Al Camy took over after a few issues and in #7 gave the Wizard a new costume. The outfit consisted of a blue tunic and tights, red shorts, and cape. The red mask was retained, along with the moustache.

Such was the state of the superhero business in the months following the debut of Superman—some interesting characters, some silly ones, but hardly more than a trickle of them. And then, in 1940, the deluge came.

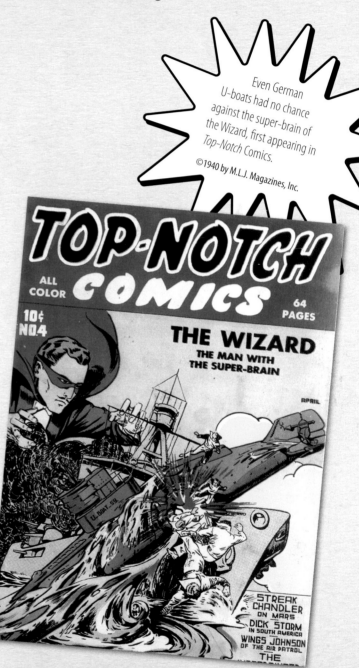

Even German U-boats had no chance against the super-brain of the Wizard, first appearing in Top-Notch Comics.

©1940 by M.L.J. Magazines, Inc.

CHAPTER 6

The Boom Years

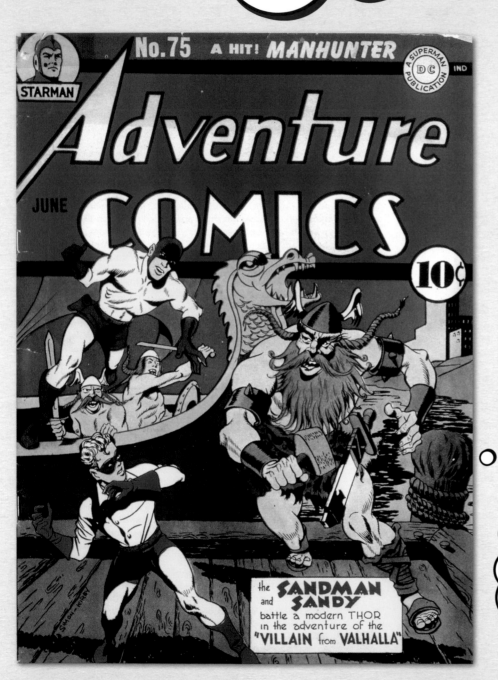

The 1940s were marked by a proliferation of superhero books after the amazing success of Superman. Scores of colorfully costumed do-gooders strode forth to combat the forces of evil. The energetic high spirits of the Golden Age of comic books are captured in this 1942 *Adventure Comics* cover by Simon and Kirby, featuring Sandman and Sandy versus Thor.

©1942 by DC Comics, Inc.

*T*he comics boom continued, not only with new titles, but with more and more publishing companies joining in. In its June 1941 issue, *Writer's Digest* exclaimed, "The number of comics on the stands continues to grow in unbelievable fashion. It is reported that there are 115 of them on the stands now, and that by September this will be increased to 135!" That was only the beginning, and hundreds more titles would come and go as the forties progressed. A few of the outfits turning out magazines had been in business at least as long as DC, but most of them were newcomers. And just about all of them did well—for a while, anyway. The most popular and best selling superhero of the decade proved to be not Superman but rather a red-clad upstart who didn't even take his profession seriously. Created by cartoonist C. C. Beck and editor-writer Bill Parker, Captain Marvel came along early in 1940. Within a very few years this beefy, perpetually grinning superhero was outselling not only Superman but also every other crime-fighter who'd followed in the wake of the Man of Steel, from Amazing Man to the Zebra.

Late in 1939 Roscoe K. Fawcett of Fawcett Publications, Inc. sent out a promotion piece to magazine distributors across the country. It announced the impending debut of *Whiz Comics*, which would star Captain

Marvel—"another character sensation in the comic field!" Until then, the Fawcett folks had been known for such magazines as *Real Life Story*, *Motion Picture*, *Mechanix Illustrated*, and *Captain Billy's Whiz-Bang*. Now they were promising wholesalers a comic book, one that was "here to stay." The forthcoming title would lead the parade and bring "permanent profits." Many comic book publishers would make similar claims and fail to live up to them, but in the case of Fawcett, all the advance hyperbole turned out to be true.

The original name selected for Fawcett's first superhero was Captain Thunder, and he was going to be the leader of a group of heroes. According to Ralph Daigh, then editorial director at Fawcett, Bill Parker's initial suggestion was "that our superhero feature a team, probably four, under the command of one hero Bill identified as Captain Thunder. The 'captain' was to have a squad of lieutenants, each possessing a singular attribute traceable to such heroes as Hercules, Atlas, Zeus, Achilles and Mercury."

In time, the group notion and the Captain Thunder name were discarded. And Parker, perhaps with suggestions from the Fawcett staff, came up with a variation on the dual identity theme— a variation that turned out to be as powerful and compelling as the dual identities of Dr. Jekyll and Mr. Hyde,

Zorro, and Superman: Captain Marvel was really a teenage boy named Billy Batson. Young readers—most of them young boy readers—loved it.

By saying the magic word "SHAZAM!" (revealed to him by a mysterious wizard in a long-forgotten section of subway), Billy could transform himself into the red-clad Captain Marvel, the World's Mightiest Mortal. Just for the record, the letters of the magic word stood for the wisdom of Solomon, the strength of Hercules, the stamina of Atlas, the power of Zeus, the courage of Achilles, and the speed of Mercury.

Despite the fact that Captain Marvel was invincible, it was Billy Batson who quietly dominated the stories. Captain Marvel was the one who duked it out with the villains, but he always returned to his true identity of Billy (by shouting "Shazam!") when the trouble had passed.

Parker's basic premise, a boy with the power to change into a full-grown superhero, was beautiful in its simplicity and inherent appeal. Youngsters were snared because the adventures were about a kid who could take a shortcut to adulthood when he needed help with a serious problem. In a sense, Billy became his own

Fawcett's Captain Marvel—known to admirers and enemies alike as the Big Red Cheese—may have been the most likable superhero of the 1940s, outselling even Superman.

©1940 by Fawcett Publications, Inc.

C.C. Beck's drawing style was simple and pleasing.

©1940 by Fawcett Publications, Inc.

In 1942, Fawcett capitalized on Captain Marvel's popularity to launch new title *Funny Animals*.

©1942 by Fawcett Publications, Inc.

CAPTAIN MARVEL JR. SINKS THE JAPS!

helpful big brother or protective father. And all it took was the magic word, not years of growing up or even months of rigorous exercise.

The captain's adventures also had great visual appeal. This was provided by Charles Clarence Beck, a young cartoonist who had been a Fawcett staff artist since the middle 1930s. A cantankerous gentleman with a strong sense of humor, he was influenced not by serious illustration but by such comic strips as *Little Orphan Annie*, *The Gumps*, and, especially, *Barney Google*. "The basis I go on is never to put in a single line that isn't necessary," he once explained. "Don't try to show off." His *Captain Marvel* stories exemplified his philosophy and were models of simplicity, clarity, and appealing design. They were as much fun to look at as they were to read.

Although Beck's friendly, cartoony style had a great deal to do with the success of the captain, he maintained, "The stories were what put Marvel over, not the drawings." And indeed, Captain Marvel's adventures were consistently well scripted, and leavened with as much wit and whimsy as action. There was nothing stuffy about the captain, who didn't seem too terribly offended whenever his enemies referred to him as "The Big Red Cheese."

Otto Binder, an established pulp science fiction writer, became the chief Captain Marvel scripter during the feature's second year. "My first *Captain Marvel Adventures* script was written in December, 1941 and appeared in the ninth issue, April, 1942," Binder once said. "The end result of this, some twelve years later in 1953, was a total of 529 stories about the Big Red Cheese alone." Binder was responsible for just about all the stories that dealt with time travel, space travel, and other science-fiction staples. He also invented Mr. Tawny, the nattily dressed talking tiger who turned out to be one of the feature's most charming and popular supporting characters.

The pulps provided Beck with not just a convivial scripter, but with with his first art assistant, as well. Pete Costanza had been a pulp illustrator before switching to comic books. "When Pete left his 'straight illustration,'" Beck said, "he turned out to be a remarkably fine cartoonist with a great sense of humor." Costanza quickly made his presence felt; his hand is already evident during the first year of *Whiz*.

As the demand for Captain Marvel stories increased—the character was appearing in *Whiz Comics* (which he shared with such stalwarts as Spy Smasher, the Golden Arrow, and Ibis the Invincible), *Captain Marvel Adventures*, and *America's Greatest* in the early 1940s— Fawcett first went to outsiders to fill the pages, and then had Beck set up a shop of his own. Among the outside artists were Jack Kirby, who produced a hurried-looking first issue of *Captain Marvel Adventures*, and George Tuska. Beck's shop employed Morris Weiss, Al Fagaly, Chic Stone, Dave Berg, Kurt Schaffenberger, and Marc Swayze.

In *Whiz* #25 another addition was made to the Marvel family. After an encounter with the odious Captain Nazi, teenage Freddy Freeman is left near death. Billy Batson decides to do something. "Deep in a forgotten section of the subway, known only to Billy himself, the boy carries his unconscious burden aboard a weird vehicle." Soon the two youths are face to face with Shazam, the wizard who had provided Billy with his alter ego nearly two years earlier—or, rather, they're face to face with Shazam's ghost, since the bearded warlock expired after performing that earlier feat. Shazam works a switch on the original trick, arranging things so that Freddy will become a superhero by shouting, "Captain Marvel!" Since this particular magic phrase isn't quite as powerful as "Shazam!" Freddy won't turn into a super adult but a super boy. Decked out in a blue version of the Marvel costume, Captain Marvel, Jr. whizzed over to *Master* Comics for a long and successful career. Mac Raboy, an impressively talented artist, drew the young hero's first adventures. It says something about how firmly the tradition of dual identity was by now established in comic books that Freddy, crippled after

his encounter with Captain Nazi, chose to return to that role when he wasn't fighting crime.

Lightning struck again at Fawcett a year later. This time it was Mary Marvel, who first flashed into being in *Captain Marvel Adventures* #18 (December 1942). Her real name was Mary Batson and she turned out to be Billy's long-lost sister. After learning her brother's secret, Mary says, "Shazam!" and—*whoom!*—she changes, too. "I feel strong—powerful," she exclaims, not at all disappointed that she's been transformed into a super teenager and not a full grown woman.

Mary, by the way, had a separate but equal version of the magic word. Whereas Billy's Shazam stands for Solomon, Hercules, Atlas, Zeus, Achilles, and Mercury, Mary's stands for Selena, Hippolyta, Ariadne, Zephyrus, Aurora, and Minerva. (It's not difficult to visualize old Shazam off in limbo somewhere, tugging at his whiskers as he works out these lists of gods and mythical figures to match the initials of his name.) Mary Marvel went on to become the leading character in *Wow Comics* with issue #9 (January 1943).

Fawcett's other early comic book titles had been more experimental. *Slam-Bang Comics*, which followed Whiz by a month, was an attempt to do a magazine without a single

costumed superhero. Instead readers were offered a lackluster lineup of plainclothes good guys—Jim Dolan, Hurricane Hansen, Lee Granger. Although a character named Diamond Jack did have a little magic going for him, he went about his business in civvies. The contents of this illfated magazine were provided by the Chesler Shop. After just seven issues, *Slam-Bang* folded.

Mary Marvel—wholesome, pretty, and dedicated to crimefighting—went solo in 1945.
©1945 by Fawcett Publications, Inc.

Master Comics was an attempt to succeed where Dell and Major Nicholson had failed and to make a success of a tabloid-sized comic book. "Now you have MASTER, the only 15c Comic Magazine!" Roscoe Fawcett told distributors. "One that makes its own Displays!—Cover . . . is 10¼ by 14 inches!—48 Big pages of 4-Color, Sure-Fire Comics." Better still, they'd make "2 cents per copy profit!" There was a superhero in this one, a blond fellow known as Master Man. Billed as the World's Greatest Hero, he was a dull fellow who didn't even have an alternate identity. Phooey! Sharing the oversized book with him were Shipwreck Roberts, the White Raja, Frontier Marshall, the Devil's Dagger, and El Carim, Master of Magic—"whose name printed backwards spells 'miracle.'"

Fawcett's ambition was apparently boundless, for the next thing the company attempted was a *weekly* comic book. Not only that—the comic would sell for just five cents. The first issue of *Nickel Comics* appeared with a May 17, 1940 cover date and the next issue appeared two weeks later. "We are able to give you a five cent comic on an every other week production schedule," explained Roscoe Fawcett to the wholesalers. "And the promise that if NICKEL COMICS clicks it will be made a weekly." Apparently, some resistance was anticipated, since several paragraphs of Fawcett's news release

struck a reassuring tone. "If we felt for one minute that a 5C comic would contribute to the detriment of the comic field, we would be foolish indeed to jeopardize the profitable one million monthly circulation now maintained on the comic publications which we distribute." (The figure of one million is explained by the Fawcett organization's distribution of magazines of other publishers.)

The featured hero in each thirty-two-page issue of *Nickel* was Bulletman. He wore a scarlet tunic, blue sash and boots, and lemon yellow riding breeches. Bulletman lived up to his name in dramatic fashion, thanks to a tapered helmet that gave him that enviable streamlined look as he flew through the air.

Despite appealing characters and innovative sizes and prices, neither *Nickel* nor *Master* succeeded, at least not in their original formats. The five-center expired after eight slim issues; the fifteen-center dropped to conventional size and price with its seventh. Bulletman replaced Master Man as *Master* cover-boy, and characters from the defunct *Slam-Bang* were also assimilated. As noted earlier, Captain Marvel, Jr. was later installed as *Master*'s leading man.

Fawcett's *Wow Comics* began life late in 1940 as a quarterly; most of the characters were leftovers from *Slam-*

Bang. The exception was Mr. Scarlet, a brand new, satanic-looking crimson avenger drawn initially by Jack Kirby. Ad copy described him this way: "Special prosecutor by day, Brian Butler discards his legal robes at midnight to become the mysterious 'Mister Scarlet,' an underworld legend—a myth who strikes with merciless reality and brings to justice those who escape the law through its legal loopholes." *Wow* eventually went monthly, added Mary Marvel to its lineup, and continued until 1948.

Fawcett's biggest hit was always Captain Marvel, but life was not easy for the red-clad Shazam-shouter. In 1941 DC Comics undertook legal action against Fawcett. DC's contention was that Captain Marvel was so close in concept to Superman that he infringed on DC's copyright. The lawsuit was fought throughout the 1940s and into the 1950s. Finally, in the middle fifties, Fawcett gave up and quit publishing Captain Marvel in any shape or form. Lawyer-comics historian Robert M. Ingersoll, writing in the *Comic's Buyer's Guide* weekly newspaper, has said, "Fawcett has sometimes been criticized for his decision to give up the fight. But it didn't really give up the fight; it had already lost it. The trial court had ruled that Captain Marvel infringed on Superman's copyright, and that issue could not be litigated again. So the

Boy Wonders

Robin the Boy Wonder teamed up with Batman in the spring of 1939, becoming the first of what was to be a long line of youthful sidekicks. In 1940 and 1941, especially, established costumed heroes and those just embarking on careers of super-altruism began showing up for work with kid companions. In the early 1950s the zealous critic of comic books, psychiatrist Dr. Fredric Wertham, would charge that "only someone ignorant of the fundamentals of psychiatry and the psychopathology of sex can fail to realize a subtle atmosphere of homoeroticism which pervades the adventures of the mature 'Batman' and his young friend 'Robin.'" Despite Wertham's observations, it seems unlikely that any of the editors who started adding boy wonders to their magazines had anything more sinister than plagiarism in mind—and an easy way to appeal to youthful readers, who could identify with the kid heroes.

Among the earliest wonder boys were Toro the Flaming Kid, who joined the Human Torch in the summer of 1940, and Roy the Super Boy, who started palling around with the Wizard at about the same time. Nicknames ending in the letter Y were especially popular and in the early 1940s Buddy, Rusty, Dusty, Speedy, and Pinky could be found teamed up with, respectively, the Eagle, Captain Aero, the Shield, Green Arrow, and Mr. Scarlet. There were also Bucky, who was Captain America's partner, and Sandy, who worked side by side with Sandman.

Now and then a certain amount of whimsy was in evidence. A minor hero called Airmale had a boy companion named Stampy, a fellow known as Nightmare worked in tandem with Sleepy. On at least one occasion the usual situation was reversed, when the pint-sized Star- Spangled Kid traveled with a lantern-jawed adult sidekick called Stripesy.

Not satisfied with just one kid companion, several heroes worked with bunches of them. The original Daredevil hung out with the Little Wise Guys and Captain Commando guided the Boy Soldiers. Joe Simon and Jack Kirby, who'd created such successful kid gangs as the Young Allies and the Boy Commandos, came up with the Newsboy Legion in 1942 and gave them a costumed adult partner known as the Guardian. Fun and lively, the kid heroes allowed the comics' young readers to cast themselves in the adventures: "If Robin can do it, so can I!"

Bulletman and, later, Bulletgirl showed up in *Nickel* and *Master* comics. The splash panel here is from *Master* #14 and was drawn by Jack Binder.

©1941 by Fawcett Publications, Inc.

Jerry Siegel and Bernard Baily's The Spectre was the most intimidating of the contemporary superheroes, as much a figure of horror as a "good guy." The Spectre meted out frightful retribution to wrongdoers, captured in this splash panel from *More Fun Comics* #57.

©1940 by DC Comics, Inc.

result of any new trial was a foregone conclusion; Fawcett would lose. Rather than spend useless time and effort fighting a losing battle, Fawcett settled out of court. An aesthetically unpopular but legally wise choice."

Captain Marvel returned to the newsstands twenty years later, under the DC banner. Artist C. C. Beck came back, too, for a while. But the captain's comeback was not exactly triumphal and Beck soon quit after an argument over scripts.

Captain Marvel's first flush of success was indicative of the public's eagerness for new superheroes. Well aware of the trend it had initiated, DC plunged more

enthusiastically into the superhero business in 1940. *More Fun* #52 (February 1940) introduced an eerie character called the Spectre. Written by Jerry Siegel and drawn by Bernard Baily, the new feature was about a redheaded cop named Jim Corrigan who, after being murdered by gangsters, returns to walk among the living as a crimebuster, cloaked in green and sporting a pasty white complexion. He had the ability, shared with Orphan Annie, of making the pupils of his eyes disappear. As all of this might suggest, the Spectre's early adventures were pretty odd. He had frequent conversations with the Almighty and

made occasional trips to the hereafter to get clues from departed souls. Once, he even stalked a supernatural villain "into the depths of infinity," a peculiar void made up mainly of clouds. He could walk through walls, turn crooks into skeletons and, on the *More Fun* covers, at least, grow as tall as a downtown office building. A grim, uniquely talented chap, the Spectre didn't just collar crooks—he enjoyed himself by *destroying* them. After one instance of brutal vigilantism, the Spectre observed, "One less vermin to peril decency."

More Fun added another weird hero a few months later, in issue #55—Dr. Fate, a Gardner Fox invention, drawn in a stylized but spooky fashion by Howard Sherman. "Dwelling apart from mankind in his lonely tower north of ghost-ridden Salem is the mysterious Dr. Fate," an early caption explained, "who called upon secret and ancient sources for the power with which he fights unusual crimes." Unusual for sure. Fate, who wore a blue and gold superhero suit and a metal helmet that completely hid his face, specialized in besting ancient Mayan gods, combating "globemen" from outer space, defeating horrors summoned from the cosmic void, and counseling young women who suspected they might be wereleopards. In one adventure with his recurrent enemy Wotan the Wizard, Fate first goes to Hell for a chat with the skeletal boatman on the River Styx and then shoots up to talk to God, who is depicted as a blinding light. Although never a top-rank hero, Dr. Fate gained a loyal coterie of fans, and remains an active character to this day.

The first honest-to-goodness superhero to grace the pages of DC's *Adventure Comics* was Bernard Baily's Hourman, who was introduced in issue #48 (March 1940). The introductory story's first caption informed readers that a young chemist named Rex "Tick-Tock" Tyler had recently discovered "Miraclo, a powerful chemical that transforms him from a meek, mild scientist to the underworld's most formidable foe . . . with Miraclo he has

for one hour the power of chained lighting-speed . . . But unless he performs his deeds of strength and daring within one hour, the effects of Miraclo wear off and the Hourman becomes his former meek self."

Adventure's next superhero was auspiciously launched in early 1941, when he got the cover and leadoff position of issue #61. This was Starman, who was quite a bit like the similarly named Skyman, who'd first taken to the air the previous year in Columbia Comics's *Big Shot Comics*. Neither had the benefit of an origin, and both were first-rate scientists who pretended to be laconic and cowardly playboys until duty called. The Skyman flew around in a super plane of his own invention; Starman flew by holding tight to his Gravity Rod—"For thousands of years men have spoken of the mysterious powers of the stars—but I am the first to discover that RADIATED STARLIGHT can be harnessed and used scientifically." The resemblances between the two heroes are accounted for by the fact that both were written by Gardner Fox.

Artwork on *Starman* was by Jack Burnley, who had been a syndicated sports cartoonist while still a teenager and an uncredited artist on *Superman* since 1940.

Despite Burnley's impressive drawing and the feature's interesting fantasy stories—in which the red-clad Starman met invisible men, mad scientists who make their victims teenie weenie, and a host of other challenging villains—he failed to live up to DC's obvious great expectations.

Starman's loss of his favored status was indicated by *Adventure* #69 (December 1941), in which the Sandman got a new look—an updated costume with yellow tunic and tights, purple cowl, cape, and boots, and a boy companion named Sandy. The artist who converted Sandman into a costumed crimebuster was Chad Grothkopf. Paul Norris drew the revised hero for the next two issues and was replaced by Joe Simon and Jack Kirby. This imaginative,

DC had high hopes for Starman, but the character failed to take hold with readers. This page is from *Adventure Comics* #67 and was drawn by Jack Burnley.

©1941 by DC Comics, Inc.

The adventures of Ultra-Man were set in the year 2239. He was only moderately popular and did not even appear on every cover.

©1939 by All-American Comics, Inc.

Green Lantern received his crimefighting abilities from a mysterious ring, drawn here by Shelly Moldoff.

©1941 by DC Comics, Inc.

The Green Lantern is one of DC's most enduring superheroes—despite a 2011 film flop. Cover art for GL's debut issue is by Howard Purcell.

©1941 by DC Comics, Inc.

very talented team proceeded to do for Sandman what they'd just done for Captain America over at Marvel; quickly, Sandman became the hit of the magazine.

Under new management and with the help of Superman and their new bunch of heroes, DC prospered. The line didn't fully assume a group identity until the spring of 1940, when DC's familiar logo, a small circle proclaiming "a DC publication," began to appear on all covers. The seal was amended to read "A Superman DC Publication" in the fall of the following year. By that time Detective Comics, Inc. was publishing well over a dozen titles. *Superman* had been added in 1939, *Batman* in 1940, and *World's Finest*, a continuation of the earlier *World's Fair* annuals, in 1941.

Late in 1938 M. C. Gaines had entered into an agreement to produce a series of comic books that would appear under the DC umbrella. The initial titles, edited by the youthful Sheldon Mayer, were *Movie Comics* and *All-American*

Comics. Both appeared the next year with cover dates of April 1939. While *All-American* featured some original material, it did not contain a single superhero and relied on newspaper reprints to fill many of its pages. Of the several characters shown on the bright yellow covers, only Mayer's Scribbly was not a newspaper reprint. The cover blurb of the first issue began by announcing, "The only comic monthly with all your old favorites: Mutt & Jeff, Ben Webster, Tippie, Reg'lar Fellers, Skippy. . . ."

Mayer once explained *All-American*'s dearth of superheroes by revealing that Gaines, despite being instrumental in the discovery of Superman, didn't believe the public would be interested in any additional superheroes. So it was that the magazine's early, original features were pretty straightforward, and reminiscent of strips that had gone before: *Red, White and Blue*, about a spy smashing trio made up of a soldier, a sailor, and a marine; *Hop Harrigan*, Jon L. Blummer's aviator strip; Adventures into the Unknown, adaptations of the juvenile science-fiction novels of Carl H. Claudy. About the closest thing to a superhero in the first year of *All-American* was Ultra-Man, a futuristic adventure strip that started in issue #8 (November 1939). Set in the United States of North America in the year 2239 and starring a heroic fellow in red tunic, green shorts, and eagle-crested metal helmet, the strip was handled by *Hop Harrigan*'s Jon L. Blummer.

All-American finally succumbed to superhero fever in the summer of 1940, when it introduced the Green Lantern in issue #16. The creation of artist Mart Nodell, with considerable help from Mayer and writer Bill Finger, GL was a hit from the start. (A good deal of the early artwork was ghosted by Irwin Hasen, who was much later involved with the Dondi newspaper strip.) Helped out by his magical power ring and Brooklynesque sidekick Doiby Dickies, Green Lantern was a hit, and (with some revision over the years) has proved to be one of the most enduring superheroes in comic book history.

Once *All-American* opened its doors to the Green Lantern, other crimefighters and superheroes began to move in. The Atom arrived in #19 (October 1940), followed by Dr. Mid-nite in #25 (April 1941) and Sargon the Sorcerer in #26 (May 1941). The cast remained stable for the next several years. Even *Mutt & Jeff*, long one of Gaines's favorites, hung around for almost the entire life of the magazine.

DC tried something new with *Movie Comics*, which began at the same time as *All-American*. *Movie Comics* offered comic book versions of current movies and used still photos with captions and balloons. It sounds appealing, but what resulted were fuzzy, poorly colored, and impossibly truncated versions of such films as *Stagecoach*, *Gunga Din*, *Son of Frankenstein*, and *A Chump At Oxford*. *Movie* died after six issues. (Fiction House launched a comic of the same title in 1946; though the films were drawn in standard comic book style, this second incarnation of *Movie Comics* lasted just four issues.)

Flash Comics premiered with the January 1940 issue. With it, DC offered two superheroes plus a masked avenger and, for good measure, a comedy character with magical powers. Edited by Sheldon Mayer, much of the magazine was written by Gardner Fox. His major creations were the Flash, also known as the Fastest Man Alive, and the winged avenger known as the Hawkman. Rounding out the early crew were the Whip, a Zorro impersonator; and Johnny Thunder, a nitwit who was looked after by a somewhat snide, anthropomorphized thunderbolt. Newspaper veteran Ed Wheelan drew another of the title's features, *Flash Picture Novelets*, which eventually became *Minute Movies*, a comic book version of his once-famous comic strip. ►

Wonder Woman & Her Sisters

A half-century after her debut, Wonder Woman remains the preeminent female crimebuster of comic books. So enduring has been her appeal that it is difficult to realize that there was a time when no comic book superheroines existed at all. In fact, there were few female characters of any kind in the original-material comic books of the 1930s.

New Fun offered Sandra of the Secret Service and *New Adventure* made room for a lady daredevil named Dale Daring. Sheena, a product of the Eisner-Iger shop, made her jungle debut in *Jumbo Comics* #1 in the summer of 1938. She wore a skimpy leopard-skin outfit—attire that wasn't considered unusual by readers who'd grown up with Tarzan. The first true costumed lady crimefighter was Lady Luck. A Will Eisner creation, she debuted in June of 1940 as a backup feature in his weekly *Spirit* newspaper comic book. Several artists drew the blonde, greenclad crimebuster over the next few years. Lady Luck had no superpowers and was similar to such male characters as the Crimson Avenger and the Green Hornet.

Wonder Woman is the greatest female crimefighter in comic book history. On this *Sensation Comics* cover by H. G. Peter, WW leads the Holliday Girls on a Halloween adventure.

©1948 by DC Comics, Inc.

The earliest costumed heroine who actually had supernatural abilities was the Black Widow, who debuted in Timely's *Mystic Comics* #4 (August 1940), billed as the "strangest, most terrifying character in action picture comics." Writer George Kapitan and artist Harry Sahle were responsible for her. The Widow dressed in a skintight black costume, gold-trimmed boots, and a green and blue cape. She had an impressive list of powers, including the ability to fly, to materialize at will, to strike her opponents dead, and to turn the pupils of her eyes into images of skulls. Rather than working on the side of law and order, the Black Widow was in the employ of Satan himself; she had died and was subsequently sent to Earth to track down sinners, kill them, and escort their souls safely to Hell. Not surprisingly, the morbid Ms. Widow didn't catch on and appeared only twice more in Mystic and two more times elsewhere.

Nineteen-forty saw few other new heroines. The Woman in Red began in *Thrilling Comics* #2 (March 1940), but a new year had begun before any further costumed ladies showed up. Among the earliest were two who signed on as companions to already established male characters. The Owl had been in *Crackajack* for several months when he was joined by Owl Girl in issue #32 (February 1941). Likewise, Bulletman was well-established by the time Bulletgirl joined him in *Master Comics* #13 (April 1941). In both instances the women were longtime friends of the heroes, and eventually discovered the heroes' true identities.

Harry Sahle gave it another try with a lady known as the Silver Scorpion, who was considerably better natured than the Black Widow. Hoodlums, unaccustomed to distaff do-gooders, tended to exclaim when they saw her—"G-gosh! It's a goil!" Introduced in Timely's *Daring Mystery Comics* #7 (April 1941), the Scorpion lasted two more issues and was gone.

Six more ladies went into business in magazines cover-dated August 1941: Miss America, Miss Victory, and Pat Patriot, as well as the Phantom Lady, the Black Cat, and Wildfire. This last character began in *Smash Comics* and possessed "the power to use flames for any purpose she desires, as a gift of the fire-god." Spider Queen, Madame Strange, and Lady Fairplay all appeared briefly in late 1940.

Dr. William Moulton Marston, a psychologist who'd lectured and taught at Radcliffe, Tufts, Columbia, and the New School of Social Research, was nearly fifty when he assumed the pen name Charles Moulton to begin scripting DC's *Wonder Woman*. The rationale he put forth makes him sound like a pioneering feminist: "Women's strong qualities have become despised because of their weak ones," he wrote. "The obvious remedy is to create a feminine character with all the strength of a superman plus all the allure of a good and beautiful woman." As to whether boys would go for a strongwoman the doctor asserted, "Give them an alluring woman stronger than themselves to submit to and they'll be proud to become her willing slaves!" Marston certainly seems to have tipped his psychosexual hand with statements like that one.

The early Wonder Woman yarns are rich with the sort of bondage and submission fantasies that had hitherto been seen only in under-the-counter publications. Moulton's scripts were some of the wackiest continuities of the era; Wonder Woman offered wartime readers a heady brew of whips, chains, and cockeyed mythology. To bring all this to life Harry G. Peter was brought in as artist. A professional cartoonist since early in the century, he gave the feature a slightly decadent, entertainingly unsavory feel. His thick pen lines, blocky figures, and Ruben-esque women added up to a unique comic-art style.

Active and fearless, Wonder Woman appealed equally to boys and girls. H. G. Peter drew the cover of her debut issue.

©1942 by DC Comics, Inc.

Bulletgirl joined Bulletman in many adventures. Cover art is by Mac Raboy.

©1941 by Fawcett Publications, Inc.

AS THE THOUGHT PRISM SHATTERS, EVERYONE IS RESTORED TO THEIR NATURAL APPEARANCE.

GREAT SHOT, STEVE! I SAW, TOO LATE, THAT **EVERYBODY** WAS BEING HYPNO-TIZED BY THAT GREEN JEWEL!

MY **THOUGHT PRISM**--I SHOULDN'T HAVE INVENTED IT!

13.

H. G. Peter's signature heavy linework gave *Wonder Woman* a substantial look.

©DC Comics, Inc.

Wonder Woman was introduced at the back of *All Star* #8 late in 1941—"At last in a world torn by the hatreds and wars of men, appears a woman to show the problems and fears of men are mere child's play." The nine-page intro story began in the manner of some of the Dorothy Lamour sarong movies of the thirties, with a handsome blond aviator crashing on the "shores of an uncharted isle set in the midst of a vast expanse of ocean." Captain Steve Trevor is seriously hurt in the crash and is nursed back to health by Diana, the daughter of the Queen of Paradise Island. The island is an all-female enclave and the Amazons have been living there, immortal, since before the Christian era. They are dedicated, because of unfortunate past experiences, to keeping "aloof from men." But the power of love proves to be too strong for Princess Di and she leaves her island and forsakes her immortality to escort Steve back to America.

When *Sensation Comics* #1 (January 1942) appeared, Wonder Woman was its leading character. She arrives in the United States with Steve, flying her transparent airplane (nobody ever explained the advantage of an invisible plane in which the pilot remains visible). WW assumes the identity of a lovelorn nurse named Diana Prince so that she can be close to Steve while he convalesces. The real Diana Prince has gone off to South America to be married. "By taking your place," she explains to the real Diana Prince, "I can see the man I love and you can marry the man you love." Suddenly, Wonder Woman sounds not quite as liberated as she had on her home turf. As with most dual identity situations, Steve never pays much attention to Diana the nurse and is enamored of Wonder Woman, whom he persists in calling "my beautiful angel."

In the second issue of *Sensation* readers met the sweets-loving Etta Candy and the girls of the Holliday College for Women. The students all seemed to attend classes wearing sweaters and shorts, but one of them criticizes Wonder Woman's costume for being too skimpy: "The Dean . . . insists on more above the waist."

Aided by Etta and the girls, Wonder Woman went on to wage war on spies, crooks, and assorted bizarre villains. There was hardly a story in which women weren't tied up with ropes, manacled with chains, and spanked. Sheldon Mayer, editor of *Sensation*, has said that the stuff would've been even wilder if he'd allowed Moulton to include all the plot elements and symbolism that the psychologist tried to sneak in.

The final Gaines-Mayer DC monthly was *Sensation Comics*. The first issue bore a January 1942 cover date and showcased a star-spangled heroine named Wonder Woman. The feature was written by psychologist William Moulton Marston under the pen name Charles Moulton and drawn by veteran illustrator Harry G. Peter. Revolutionary in a quiet way, Wonder Woman demonstrated that a woman could be every bit as heroic as a man.

Among the other characters in *Sensation* were Mr. Terrific, the Gay Ghost, and Little Boy Blue. One of the more novel characters was Hasen and Finger's Wildcat, a boxing champ who donned an animal skin to fight crime.

One of Sheldon Mayer's more enduring inventions was *All Star Comics*. Originally a quarterly, it brought together characters from both the DC and M. C. Gaines's old All American branches of the family. The bright yellow cover of the first issue, showing panels ripped from four of the strips, was designed by Mayer, who also drew the lively, star-spangled logo. In issue #3 (Winter 1940) the first meeting of the Justice Society of America (JSA) was held—with Sandman, the Atom, the Spectre, the Flash, Hawkman, Dr. Fate, the Green Lantern, and Hourman attending.

All Star #4, the first bimonthly issue, was also the first to feature a unifying theme that ran through all the stories. As devised by the inventive Gardner Fox, novel-length JSA adventures were divided into separate chapters, each featuring a particular hero; each hero's regular artist illustrated that chapter. From then on, the JSA teamed up in each issue to travel to other planets, defend the country against spies, feed the starving peoples of Europe, and defeat an impressive assortment of villains such as the Brain Wave, the Psycho-Pirate, and Degaton. By defying the conventional wisdom that kids don't like groups of heroes, *All Star*'s JSA concept paved the way for numberless superhero groups.

Not everything at DC was superhero-oriented. Like Major Nicholson before him, M. C. Gaines had a yearning to educate as well as entertain. As implemented by Nicholson, this yearning resulted in adaptations of the classics in *More Fun* and *New Adventure*. In Gaines's case, the result was *Picture Stories From the Bible*. The first issue appeared in 1942, with art by Don Cameron. Mayer never thought much of the project and tried to have as little to do with the project as possible. But Gaines was determined to make the idea work, and followed his first title with *Picture Stories from American History*, in 1946. By the time *Picture Stories from World History* appeared in 1947, Gaines had parted with DC and founded his own EC line. Mayer stayed on at DC, stepping down as an editor in 1948 but continuing to draw for the company.

Late in 1939 pulp publisher Martin Goodman ventured into comic books. He called his outfit Timely Publications and the first issue of his new magazine was just plain *Marvel Comics*. While everything that the Funnies, Inc. shop dreamed up for the premiere issue wasn't first-rate, they did manage to include the Human Torch, Sub-Mariner, the Angel, and the jungleman Ka-Zar.

As discussed in Chapter Five, *Marvel Comics* became *Marvel Mystery Comics* with the second issue. To most fans the magazine was always simply *Marvel* and it is the cornerstone of today's large Marvel Comics empire.

Timely introduced other titles, including *Daring Mystery Comics* and *Mystic Comics*, but never settled on a stable cast of characters. Over the ensuing months the publisher's heroes included the Fiery Mask, the Laughing Mask, the Phantom Bullet, Zephyr Jones and his Rocket Ship, Trojak the Tigerman, the Marvel Boy, the Thunderer, the Fin (another aquatic hero by Bill Everett, creator of Sub-Mariner), Blue Diamond, the Silver Scorpion, Citizen V, the Falcon, Blue Blaze, Dynamic Man, Flexo the Rubber Man, the Black Marvel, Super Slave, the Blazing Skull, and the Destroyer. This lengthy roster of colorful heroes kept Timely's arists and writers busy, but did not inspire long-lasting reader interest.

The situation changed in 1941, when Timely introduced Captain America. Until Cap's debut in 1941, characters who got whole comic books of their own had first had a successful tryout elsewhere— Superman in *Action Comics*, Batman in *Detective Comics*, Captain Marvel in *Whiz*. Captain America was the exception, cooked up for Timely by the recently formed team of Joe Simon and Jack Kirby and introduced to the world

in *Captain America Comics* #1. "Captain America was created for a time that needed noble figures," Kirby once recalled. "We weren't at war yet, but everyone knew it was coming. That's why Captain America was born; America needed a superpatriot." As to their new hero's appearance, Kirby said, "Drape the flag on anything, and it looks good. We gave him a chain mail shirt and shield, like a modern-day crusader. The wings on his helmet were from Mercury. . . . He symbolized the American dream." Obviously a superhero with that much going for him couldn't fail. Indeed, Captain America was a smash hit right from the start. The first issue provided not only his origin but also introduced Bucky, his boy companion.

Kirby had a good deal of help with the art chores. Simon did some of the inking, but penciling and inking were also handled by A1 Avison, Syd Shores, and Reed Crandall. Still, the book's visual tone really came from Kirby, whose flair for dynamic action and fluid anatomy set the tone not just for *Captain America*, but for two generations of superhero artists.

Kirby thought big; one identifying trademark of the art he did for Cap was his love of spacious panels

Sub-Mariner first appeared in *Marvel Comics* and graduated to his own title.

©1947 by Manvis Publications

Captain America's patriotic adventures from the war years are thrilling and memorable. This typically frenetic cover was drawn by Alex Schomburg.

©1945 by Complete Photo Story Corp.

Captain America's most frightening nemesis was the Red Skull: murderer, betrayer, and Nazi.

©1941 by Timely Comics

that often stretched across two pages. "Movies were what I knew best," Kirby has said, "and I wanted to tell stories the way they do." When Simon and Kirby were lured over to DC, the Captain and Bucky were taken over by Avison, Shores, and others.

Throughout the magazine's glory days during World War II, its colorful, actionful covers made it instantly recognizable. Simon and Kirby set the style with the covers of the book's earliest issues, which placed Cap and Bucky in the midst of a wild variety of Axis death traps. They were menaced by stretch rack, fire, crushing, stabbing, and numerous other horrific methods. Throughout 1942, Al Avison's flair for the grotesque manifested itself in a cover gallery of fiendish Nazi hunchbacks and inhuman Japanese dwarfs. These howling fiends enjoyed their work, but then, Cap and Bucky enjoyed theirs, too!

Many of the best *Captain America* covers were by Alex Schomburg, a versatile artist who painted serious works in the contemplative style of Thomas Hart Benton,

but who drew comic book covers with wild abandon. As depicted by Schomburg, Cap and Bucky pursue evil by leaping from tram cars, locomotives, and the roofs of buildings. In scenes in which every bit of cover space is filled with hurtling figures, the pair slug it out with saboteurs, fifth columnists, gorillas, even Hitler himself. Inside and out, then, *Captain America* summed up all the energy and reckless fun of comics in the forties.

Captain America wasn't Timely's only success. The company put together a popular ensemble when it mixed a little of the Justice Society idea with Hollywood's Dead End Kids concept, to come up with the Young Allies. The first issue of the group's quarterly was published in the summer of 1941. The story filled the whole book and teamed Bucky and Toro—the Human Torch's boy pal—with three everyday kids—Knuckles, "formerly a dead-end kid," a fat boy named Tubby, and a black youth, Whitewash ("Yeah man! I is also good on de watermelon!") Well, what the comic lacked in racial understanding it tried to make up for with action. In the first story, the Young Allies join forces with a British secret agent, do combat with the formidable Red Skull, and even have a brush with Hitler in Berlin. At the end, after Captain America and the Human Torch have lent a hand, readers were asked, "Do you want to see more of the Young Allies?" The response was positive and the "small band of daring kids" went on to appear in twenty issues of their own magazine as well as in *Kid Komics*, *Amazing*, *Mystic*, and *Marvel*. As with

Rowdy-yet-patriotic kid gangs were a staple of wartime comics. Timely's *Young Allies* was a particularly action-packed example. Simon and Kirby drew the debut cover (above); Alex Schomburg drew the cover of issue #8 (right).

©1941, 1943 by USA Publications

Three of Timely's greatest superheroes—along with some also-rans—appeared on the debut of *All Winners*.

©1941 by Comic Magazine Corp.

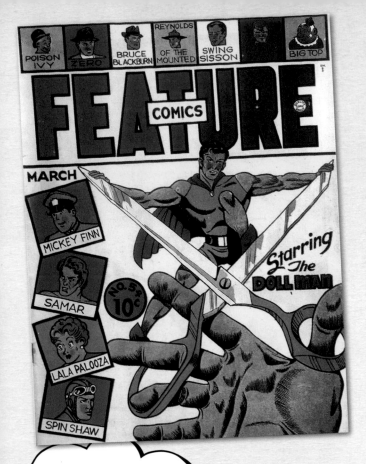

Captain America, Young Allies was distinguished by fast, improbable action and wild covers by Simon and Kirby, Alex Schomburg, and Al Gabrielle.

The summer of '41 also brought Timely's answer to DC's *All Star: All Winners.* Unfortunately, the new magazine had to fudge a bit to come up with five heroes who could be labeled winners. Undoubtedly the Human Torch, Sub-Mariner, and Captain America fit the bill, but the Angel was a second stringer

and the Black Marvel was known only to the few readers who had happened to notice him in the sporadically printed issues of *Mystic.* He was replaced in the second issue by the Destroyer and the oddly named Whizzer, a fellow who'd gained his super speed by way of a transfusion of mongoose blood.

Not until 1946 did Timely get around to imitating the Justice Society. At that time, it introduced a group known as the All Winners Squad. Consisting of the Human Torch, Sub-Mariner, Captain America, the Whizzer, and a lady known as Miss America, the squad had two book-length adventures, in *All Winners* #19 and #21 (there was no *All Winners* #20).

The country's fervent interest in superheroes meant that there was no dearth of entrepreneurs who wanted a piece of the comic book action that had been staked out by DC and Timely. One of them, Everett M. "Busy" Arnold, was a graduate of Brown University and had worked in the printing business since leaving college. He'd printed the Cook-Mahon Comics Magazine titles (see Chapter Three) and in 1937 went into publishing himself. Possibly made cautious by the far from conspicuous success of Cook and Mahon's *Funny Pages* and *Funny*

Picture Stories, Arnold made sure he had solvent partners in his own attempt. These included Frank J. Markey, who was an executive with the McNaught Syndicate and also ran a subsidiary syndicate using his own name, and the Cowles family. These latter worthies owned the Register & Tribune Syndicate, the Des Moines newspaper of that name, and *Look* magazine. For his editor

Arnold brought in a cartoonist named Ed Cronin. Arnold called his company the Quality Comics Group, and his first title was *Feature Funnies*, a good example of the effect of the appearance and subsequent success of Superman. The comic book began life in the autumn of 1937 and was devoted mainly to reprinting newspaper strips. By early 1940 it had changed its name to *Feature Comics* and was showcasing a superhero of its own on the covers. This hero was a diminutive do-gooder known as Doll Man, created by Will Eisner and drawn in his earliest adventures by Lou Fine.

Quality's first companion to *Feature* came along in the summer of 1939, and was called *Smash Comics*. Despite the fact that *Smash* went on sale a year after *Action Comics* and was made up entirely of original material, the first issue had no superheroes. The closest thing was a robot named Bozo, the invention of a diligent but second-rate artist named George Brenner. Finally, in the fourteenth issue, the Ray arrived. Described as the "new sensation of the comic magazines," he had mysterious powers that included the ability to fly, to materialize out of a beam of light, and to convert himself by mystical means from a business-suited newsman to a yellow-costumed hero. The stories weren't especially compelling, alternating between crook sequences and fantasies

involving pirates and monster-ridden castles, but Lou Fine's impressive artwork made the Ray worth following.

Despite his less than terrific storylines, the Ray might have remained the head man in *Smash Comics* had not a supremely inventive artist named Jack Cole come along with Midnight in *Smash* #18 (January 1941). Midnight—a character with physical similarities to Will Eisner's The Spirit—was a crimefighter who went to work wearing a suit, a fedora, and a domino mask. Cole's layouts were bold and unconventional, utilizing incredible long shots, overhead shots, close-ups, and other approaches that utilized the framing tricks of action movies and animated cartoons. Cole also had a strong and active sense of humor. He never took anything too seriously in his hero strips, including violence, death, and vast destruction.

By 1940, America's newsstands were becoming crowded with comic books. There still was room for more, however, so Quality introduced three new titles—and a new batch of super heroes and heroines. Counted among these new characters were a superpatriot, a man who could fly like a bird, a woman cop . . . and the only female impersonator in comic books.

Lou Fine was a mainstay of the Quality Comics staff through the 1940s, including the thoughtfully drawn Black Condor.

©1942 by Comic Magazine, Inc.

The first of the new Quality titles, the explosively titled *Crack Comics*, appeared in the spring of 1940. Its features included *The Space Legion*, *The Red Torpedo*, and an old Cook-Mahon character, *The Clock*, who was having another go-round in comics. Artist Paul Gustavson contributed *Alias the Spider*, featuring an archer who fought crime and lawlessness with "his deadly bow." *Crack*'s most unusual strip, *Madam Fatal*, dealt with a famous character actor who dressed up like a little old lady to go after crooks. Crimebusting of the more familiar sort was provided by the Black Condor, a sturdy superhero whose dark blue costume included a cape that could be made to look like wings. In his youth he'd picked up the ability to fly and he used that ability in his war on crime. The most attractive thing about the feature was, as with the Ray, Lou Fine's art.

The first issue of Quality's *National Comics*, aptly enough, had a patriotic cover date of July 1940. Its star was Uncle Sam, enlisted from political cartoons and recruiting posters to fill a new role: superhero. Uncle Sam was billed on the cover as "America's Greatest Comic Character." The contents of *National* came from the Eisner-Iger shop; Eisner himself drew the "9 action packed pages" that introduced Uncle Sam. Besides Uncle Sam, the new magazine offered such strips as *Prop Powers*, featuring a daredevil pilot; *Sally O'Neil*, concerning a pretty brunette policewoman; *Merlin the Magician*, which dealt with an idle playboy who inherits the cloak of the original Arthurian Merlin and becomes a dedicated super magician; *Wonder Boy*, who comes to earth "from the vacuous depths of outer space" and uses his "strength of a thousand men" to work as the first teenage superhero in comics; *Pen Miller*, starring a "famous comic magazine cartoonist who is also an amateur detective of wide reputation"; and *Kid Patrol*, a crimefighting variation of Hollywood's Our Gang (Little Rascals) concept.

Hit Comics arrived in the same month as *National* but never managed to live up to its name. The book had a dozen characters but not one was a winner. The leadoff story dealt with a blond good guy called Hercules. Then there was the Red Bee. The degree of seriousness involved with this character was best indicated by the pen name attached to it: B. H. Apiary. Any kid who knew what an apiary was could guess that the gentleman's initials must stand for Bee Hive. In real life the Bee was Rick Raleigh, an assistant DA in crime-infested Superior City. Impatient with the delays of the law, he decided to undertake a "one man fight on crime." Concealed in the buckle of his belt was a trained bumblebee, who came buzzing out on cue to sting criminals. A novel concept, yes, but not one that was destined to excite many readers.

The last two Quality monthlies bowed side by side in the summer of 1941. *Police Comics* #1 featured "the mysterious figure who fights for justice as the Firebrand." Fred Guardineer contributed *The Mouthpiece*, about

During World War II, Quality turned Uncle Sam into a barrel-chested superhero, with art by Lou Fine.

©1941 by Comic Magazine, Inc.

Plastic Man's remarkable physical abilities delighted readers and allowed creator Jack Cole to liberally apply humor.

©1948 by Comic Magazines

Jack Cole used Plastic Man to send up Americans' indulgent, nostalgic view of the 1890s on the cover of *Plastic Man* #2.

©1944 by Vital Publications, Inc.

"newly elected District Attorney, young Bill Perkins," who wore a black mask along with his business suit to go after "evasive figures beyond the law." Unlike most of the comic books of the period, *Police* found room for a woman character. "The society columns record the activities of Sandra Knight, debutante daughter of Senator Henry Knight. . . ." No one suspected that the frivolous Sandra was also the fabulous Phantom Lady, whose battles against spies and public enemies constantly made the headlines.

Plastic Man began his career in the middle of the first issue of *Police*. Another creation of Jack Cole, the red-suited rubberman had only six pages in which to introduce himself, get through the obligatory origin, and establish himself with the reader. He did an impressive job and by issue #5 he was also appearing on the covers. Readers loved the character's uninhibited physicality—he could elongate his fingers and turn them into the bars of a cage; he could flatten his body and skim through the sky like a kite; he could even bounce across the ground like a rubber ball. By *Police* #9 Plas had ousted Firebrand from the title's lead spot and had nine pages to himself. Less than six months after that poor Firebrand had departed and Cole's flexible hero had thirteen pages. Little wonder, for Cole had a strong sense of

what the fast-growing new comic book business was all about. He knew how to package his work and how to communicate directly with the reader. Indeed, there is a freshness and an immediacy about Cole's Plastic Man that is matched by very few characters of the era. Wildly exaggerated, howlingly funny, and unafraid to bend the sometimes stolid "rules" of the superhero genre, Plastic Man is one of comics' alltime great creations.

During his heyday Plastic Man's only real competition came from the Spirit. Will Eisner's streetwise masked man first appeared in *Police* #11 (September 1942). The character was already two years old by that time, since the weekly *Spirit* booklets had first appeared in newspaper Sunday comic sections in June of 1940. For the comic book reprint of the first story, by the way, Eisner added the Spirit's domino mask to the full-face title panel portrait; he'd left that out the first time around. That initial episode was the origin story, but from then on the stories were not reprinted in sequence.

The Spirit was a strip of great inventiveness, distinguished by Eisner's moody, shadowed drawings (strongly reminiscent of Hollywood *film noir* crime thrillers), and by his flair for affecting, often bizarre characterizations, plot, and dialogue. If Orson Welles had been a comic strip artist, he might have created The Spirit.

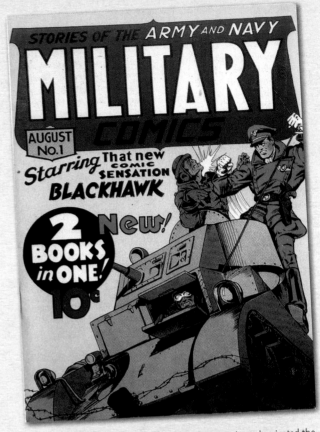

The indominatable Blackhawk, the only Polish superhero, dominated the pages of Quality's *Military Comics*. Blackhawk remains popular to this day. The cover of *Military* #1 was drawn by Blackhawk creator Will Eisner.

©1941 by Comic Magazines, Inc.

Quality's *Military Comics* was launched just a few months before the United States entered World War II. The magazine was edited by Eisner, who'd ended his partnership with Jerry Iger to start a shop of his own, and offered its readers "Stories of the Army and Navy." That cover slogan was rather loosely interpreted and some fairly unconventional warriors were to be found doing battle within.

The undisputed star of *Military* was Blackhawk. Created by Eisner and drawn

Alex Schomburg drew the covers for *Thrilling* #59 (top) and #11. Doc Strange owed his amazing powers to a chemical compound called Alosun.

©1947, 1940 by Better Publications, Inc.

by Charles "Chuck" Cuidera, he had the leadoff slot in every issue. In the first adventure readers learned that Blackhawk was a Polish aviator whose brother and sister had been killed by the Nazis. Escaping his occupied homeland, he acquired a mysterious island to use as a base. There, he recruited a band of freedom-minded outcasts and fugitives to carry on aerial guerilla warfare against Nazi Germany. With *Military* #12 Reed Crandall, with an assist from Alex Kotzky in that issue only, took over the drawing. A gifted draftsman with a keen sense of drama, Crandall was one of the best comic book illustrators of the period. Although adept at any genre, he seemed more at home with the Blackhawk crew than he had with any of the superheroes Quality had saddled him with. Crandall's *Blackhawk* work is excellent and he remained with the feature, off and on, for the next several years.

Military Comics offered a lot more than just *Blackhawk*. The title also featured *Loops and Banks*, about a team of flyers; *Shot and Shell*, concerning a big blond hayseed pilot teamed with a diminutive con man named Colonel Shot; and *The Blue Tracer*, about a super plane that was the "newest and earliest flying engineer of war."

Military also featured *Death Patrol*, brightly written and drawn by Jack Cole. The strip dealt with "five convicts and one Del Van Dyne, former airlines pilot, thrown together by fate. They fly to England and fight for the RAF! THE DEATH PATROL,

most daring of all British warbirds!" The group came by its nickname because in each of the earliest adventures one of them was killed and replaced by a new recruit. Cole turned out only three stories before turning things over to Dave Berg, an artist-writer who found popularity many years later with his "The Lighter Side of . . ." feature in *Mad* magazine.

The fullness of the *Military* lineup makes clear that one of the biggest differences between today's comics and those of a half-century ago is the number of features. Nowadays there is usually only one character, or a single team of characters, in each issue of a comic book. But in the old days a selection of anywhere from eight to a dozen separately featured characters was typical. All comic books boasted sixty-four pages (today's standard is thirty-two) and individual stories ran from four pages to thirteen.

As profits increased more and more publishers hopped onto the comic book bandwagon. One of them was Ned Pines, who had entered publishing in the 1920s. In the 1930s he and his editor-in-chief, Leo Margulies, were running the Thrilling Group of pulp magazines. Pines's list of pulp titles was a long one that included *Phantom Detective*, *Thrilling Detective*, *Thrilling Love*, *Thrilling Western*, *Startling Stories*, *Thrilling Wonder Stories*, *Black Book Detective*, and *The Rio Kid*. The Pines outfit also published *Screenland*, *Silver Screen*, and *Your Daily Horoscope*. Pines wanted to get into ▶

Superpatriots

The United States officially entered the Second World War in December of 1941, following the Japanese attack on the U.S. naval base at Pearl Harbor, Hawaii. In the tense years leading up to that event, as war jitters increased, over two dozen superpatriotic heroes and heroines showed up in American comic books. All wore costumes that utilized the stars and stripes in their design, all fought spies, saboteurs, and would-be invaders. The concerns of Americans— especially kid readers—as Hitler's war spread across Europe were reflected in comic books and especially in superpatriotic features.

As the 1930s ended, America was swept by a growing patriotic fervor. "Americans had dragged their patriotism out of the closet," reported *Life* in its July 22, 1940 issue, "and were wearing it in the streets as they had not done since 1918. Every musical show on Broadway featured the national anthem as a curtain-raiser or finale. Red, white and blue gallantly gleamed on lapels, umbrellas, hats and suspenders. Patriotic pins, pendants, clips and bracelets 'walked off the counters' of department and five-and-dime stores as fast as they could be stocked."

The Selective Service Act, better known as the draft, was passed in the autumn of 1940. Undoubtedly it was of more interest to the young writers and artists producing the comic book stories than to most of their readers. Many of the creators now had to face the possibility of being put into uniform—a khaki, or maybe navy blue, uniform and not one that was emblazoned with stars and stripes and accented by a flowing cape. That comic book creators grasped the reality of being drafted may account for the fact that some of the comic book superpatriots didn't exactly volunteer for their jobs.

The first superpatriotic hero was the Shield, who did volunteer. His star-spangled costume, adapted from the flag, set the style for what the well-dressed ultrapatriotic superhero should wear. Created by Harry Shorten and Irv Novick, he debuted in MLJ's *Pep Comics* #1 (January 1940). His avowed purpose was to "shield the U.S. government from all enemies." He was followed by Uncle Sam, who appeared in Quality's *National Comics*. Thanks to creator Will Eisner, the comic book Uncle Sam was a muscular superman rather than the aging, avuncular fellow most people knew from billboards and recruiting posters.

Next came Minute-Man, who debuted in Fawcett's *Master Comics* #11 (February 1941). After being drafted into the Army, Jack Weston is asked by his guardian, General Milton, to combat "an enemy who strikes from within. Sabotage and wholesale destruction will follow in the wake of the draft. To combat that I have chosen you. You are strong, brave and alert. You'll be more than a soldier. You'll be a MINUTE-MAN." No superpowers went with the job, but Jack got a red, white, and blue star-spangled costume that he wore beneath his Army private uniform. Dubbed the "One Man Army," Minute-Man specialized in fighting the usual assortment of spies, saboteurs, and foreign invaders.

Captain America also entered the field early in 1941, in his own magazine. His alter-ego, blond Steve Rogers, tries to enlist in the service but is turned down "because of his unfit condition." It isn't clear in the introductory episode whether he willingly takes an experimental injection from Professor Reinstein, but he does seem to go along with Reinstein's scheme to create a super-soldier. The "strange seething liquid" works like a magical Charles Atlas course and turns Rogers from a 97-pound weakling into a superhuman. Reinstein has envisioned a "corps of super-agents whose mental and physical ability will make them a terror to spies and saboteurs!" But the prof is gunned down by a Gestapo agent after creating just one superman, who takes the name Captain America.

It would seem, if you think about it at all, that carrying on a double life while a private in the United States Army would be extremely difficult. Nonetheless Rogers, like Jack (Minute-Man) Weston, tried just that. He pulled it off, too, and even met Bucky Barnes, an energetic, fearless youngster who's described as the "mascot of the regiment." The two teamed up against the "vicious elements who seek to overthrow the U.S. government!"

Several women became superpatriots in 1941. A lady named USA, the Spirit of Old Glory, commenced her brief career in Quality's *Feature Comics* #42 (March 1941). She wasn't exactly a person, but rather a sort of mystical figure who personified the spirit of the American flag. A blonde in a short, blue dress, she carried a large flag that was able to flutter on its own. When it didn't, that meant trouble and prompted USA to utter the memorable line, "My flag droops . . . danger lurks!" The danger might be a subversive school teacher or an invasion by a foreign army decked out in purple uniforms. USA was a novel character, but she had just seven adventures.

Quality tried again with Miss America, who bowed in *Military Comics* #1 (August 1941). A similarly named heroine, Miss Victory, showed up in the first issue of Holyoke's *Captain Fearless* (August 1941). Over at Lev Gleason, Pat Patriot was working in an aircraft factory when, suspecting her bosses of sabotage, she donned a red, white, and blue costume and became "America's Joan of Arc." She appeared in *Daredevil* from #2 (August 1941) through #11 (June 1942). The very talented Reed Crandall was the first of several artists to draw Pat's adventures.

Male superpatriots continued to proliferate during 1941. Captain Battle was the invention of Jack Binder and various members of his art and editorial shop. The captain, who first appeared in Lev Gleason's *Silver Streak Comics* #10 (May 1941), stood out from all the others because he wore a black patch over his left eye. As his origin story explained, the captain had been the youngest combatant in World War I, and had lost his eye in battle. According to an introductory caption, Battle "has given his life to the scientific perfection of inventions which he uses to overcome evil and aggressive influences. His curvoscope, his luceflyer and his dissolvo give him power possessed by no other mortal alive." Captain Battle was armed for bear, and a good thing, too, for he coped with somewhat more exotic villainy than that faced by his colleagues. In his initial adventure he notes some strange doings in Europe by way of his curvoscope, a telescope that "allows him to see anywhere on Earth, because its lenses follow the Earth's curves." It seems a race of giant birdmen is invading Europe. Captain Battle races over there in his luceflyer, which travels at "almost the speed of light," and defeats the plan.

Marvel offered two superpatriots in *U.S.A. Comics*, the Defender and Mr. Liberty, and added the Patriot to *Marvel Mystery Comics* after the character had tried out in the Human Torch's magazine. Among the others from various publishers were Captain Courageous, the Conqueror, Man of War, the Lone Warrior, Captain Freedom, Captain Flag, the Stars and Stripes (a patriotic trio), the Flag, Flagman, Major Victory, the Fighting Yank, Stormy Foster, the Great Defender, Yankee Doodle Jones, U.S. Jones, and the Star-Spangled Kid. Ironically, few new superpatriots were introduced after America actually entered the war.

Adolf Hitler turned up on an occasional comic book cover but never so vividly as here on *Daredevil* #1. Art is by Bob Wood and Charles Biro.

©1941 by Your Guide

Captain Battle (left) used an amazing array of inventions in his unceasing battle for "freedom and decency," with art by Jack Binder. The Eagle (right) laughs off Nazi machine-gun fire on the cover of his first solo issue.

©1941 by New Friday Publications, Inc.

comic books. After a false start in 1939–40 with *Best Comics*, an eccentric, oversized magazine that had to be read sideways, Pines issued a more conventional title cover-dated February 1940. It was called, as might have been expected, *Thrilling Comics*. This was followed by *Exciting Comics* and *Startling Comics*.

Half of the first issue of *Thrilling* was devoted to the origin of Dr. Strange (not to be confused with the later Marvel mystery man). Created by writer Richard Hughes and drawn initially by Alexander Kostuk, Strange was a gifted scientist who'd invented a compound called Alosun. This elixir endowed him with a wide range of powers, including "the ability to soar through the air as if winged." Before too long, no doubt under the influence of pulp hero Doc Savage, he changed his name to Doc Strange. He subsequently shed his civilian suits for a costume consisting of boots, red T-shirt, and blue riding breeches. Doc Strange was joined in *Thrilling* by the Ghost, the Rio Kid, and the Woman in Red.

Pines's next title, *Exciting Comics*, debuted with an April 1940 cover date, and offered a mix of features that included *The Space Rovers*. This science fiction opus was drawn, anonymously, by Max Plaisted, one of the leading illustrators of the *Spicy Detective* pulp. In its ninth issue (May 1941) *Exciting* introduced the Black Terror, yet another

superhero who got his powers from a magic potion—"Bob Benton discovers titanic strength in a solution of formic ethers!" The science might have been shaky, but with his black hair, black domino mask, blue and red cape, and black costume adorned on its chest with a white skull and crossbones, the Black Terror was certainly one of the more intimidating-appearing of all the early superheroes.

Startling Comics originally starred Captain Future, who bore no resemblance to the Pines pulp hero of the same name. In issue #10 (September 1941) a super-patriot called the Fighting Yank was installed as the leading hero. Other characters included the Masked Rider; Mystico; and Biff Powers, Big Game Hunter.

Another important company to join the fray in this period was MLJ. Less formal than the movie studio MGM, the MLJ company took its name from the first-name initials of its proprietors, who had backgrounds in the pulps and in magazine distribution. They were Morris Coyne, Louis Silverkleit, and John Goldwater, who entered the burgeoning funny book field together at the end of 1939. The artwork and scripts for the earliest issues of their new titles were provided by the Harry "A" Chesler shop. While talented people did work for Chesler, it's evident he didn't send in his first team to turn out material for

Morris, Louis, and John; the MLJ line got off to a rather shaky start with *Blue Ribbon Comics*. The first issue bore a November 1939 cover date and its star was not a costumed hero but a dog. Rang-A-Tang, billed as the Wonder Dog, gnaws on a villain's wrist on the cover and leads off the issue with a six-page adventure. *Blue Ribbon's* first superhero appeared in the second issue. He wore a green costume, a green cowl with wings over the ears, and a scarlet cape. His name was Bob Phantom, which isn't a particularly striking name for a fellow who fancied himself "the Scourge of the Underworld." A crimefighter with a first name is just too folksy to strike terror in crooked hearts. (How do you suppose

Rang-a-Tang the Wonder Dog was the original star of MLH's *Blue Ribbon Comics*. Cover art for issue #8 was drawn by Ed Smalle.

bad guys would react to Bill Batman or Fred Superman?)

Artist Charles Biro—soon to become a major force in the industry—was the most talented contributor to the second issue of *Blue Ribbon*. His *Scoop Cody*, dealing with an ace newsman, ended after two issues, but *Corporal Collins*, about a "two-fisted American in the French infantry," fared somewhat better.

MLJ quickly wised up to the poor quality of work that the Chesler shop had provided. The company quit Chesler and hired some of his better staffers away from him. *Blue Ribbon* #4 (June 1940) introduced a batch of new characters, including Hercules, the Fox, the Green Falcon, and Ty-Gor. The ninth issue (February 1941) signed on Mr. Justice. Created by writer Joe Blair and artist Sam Cooper, he was, like DC's Spectre, dead. And like the Spectre, Mr. Justice had those blankly staring, Orphan Annie eyes. Off duty, his peepers reverted to normalcy and he assumed "the form of a mortal man," a handsome blond fellow in a conservative business suit. *Blue Ribbon*'s last hero, Captain Flag, bowed in issue #16 (September 1941).

The second MLJ title was *Top-Notch Comics*, and only one superhero was dreamed up for its December 1939 debut issue—the Wizard, the fellow with the Super Brain. Bob Phantom became part of the cast in issue #3. The Firefly, creation of writer Harry Shorten and

artist Bob Wood, was added in #8 and in #9 (October 1940) came the Black Hood, another of those impatient officers of the law who became a vigilante. In addition to the intimidating hood that give him his name, he wore a yellow tunic, black shorts, and yellow tights.

In the summer of 1942 *Top-Notch* converted to humor. With the bold slogan, "We dared to do it!! A Joke Book That's Really Funny!" issue #28 appeared under the revised title *Top-Notch Laugh*. The Black Hood stayed on for a time but most of the other heroes were dumped and replaced by allegedly funny stuff the caliber of *Dotty and Ditto*, *Pokey Oakey*, and *Senor Siesta*.

MLJ's *Pep Comics* had a January 1940 cover date on its first issue. At the outset, the magazine boasted two superheroes— one of them, the Shield, was the first of that breed of comic book superpatriots who wore red, white and blue. Harry Shorten was the scriptwriter and Irving Novick the artist on these adventures of "the G-Man Extraordinary." *Pep*'s other super-powered character was Jack Cole's the Comet. When the Comet was killed by gangsters' bullets, his brother, the Hangman, replaced him in issue #17.

The MLJ folks inaugurated their fourth and last monthly as 1940 was starting. Over at *Action Comics*, Superman was

The Shield & Dusty team up with Hangman on the cover of *Pep Comics* #8, drawn by Irv Novick.

©1941 by M.L.J. Magazines, Inc.

Bob Montana, the creator of Archie, drew the cover for *Top-Notch* Laugh #30 when MLJ had temporarily given up on superheroes.

©1942 by M.L.J. Magazines, Inc.

known as the Man of Steel, but that didn't bother the upstart of *Zip Comics*, Steel Sterling. A red-costumed, abundantly muscled fellow, the character was a joint effort by artist Charles Biro and the magazine's editor, Abner Sundell. Since Biro had been doing cute comedy fillers until a few months earlier, he still was not completely at home with straight adventure. But he had a strong sense of action and his

Joe Simon and Jack Kirby illustrated the Black Owl for *Prize Comics*. This page is from *Prize #9*.

©1940 by Feature Publications

The faintly menacing Green Lama was a terror to crooks everywhere.

©1940 by Feature Publications, Inc.

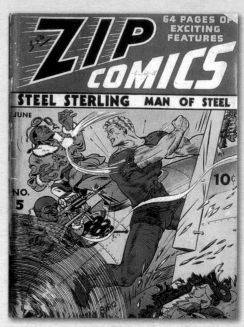

Steel Sterling was artist Charles Biro's first attempt at a "serious" feature, seen here on *Zip Comics*.

©1940 by M.L.J. Magazines, Inc.

early pages, though often crudely drawn, had movement and life. Throughout his career, in fact, Biro's potent techniques for grabbing and holding the readers' attention would always be several paces ahead of his actual drawing ability. Besides Steel Sterling, *Zip* offered other costumed heroes—Scarlet Avenger, Mr. Satan, Black Jack, and the Web.

The deluge of new companies and new titles continued through the early forties. Crestwood offered Prize Comics, with the Black Owl, the Green Lama, and Dick Briefer's Frankenstein. Vincent Sullivan left DC to edit Columbia Comics's *Big Shot Comics*, the home of Skyman, the Face, and Sparky Watts. The Hillman Company, a pioneer in paperback books, introduced Air Fighters starring

"America's Ace," Airboy. The Harvey Brothers were responsible for *Speed Comics*, *Green Hornet*, and *Champ* and such characters as Captain Freedom, Shock Gibson, and the Black Cat, the last a long-legged beauty who was one of the most successful of lady crimefighters. The Curtis Publishing Company of Philadelphia, publisher of both the *Saturday Evening Post* and *Ladies Home Journal*, unobtrusively went into the comics business in 1940, too. Calling itself Novelty Press, Inc. and operating out of editorial offices on West 52nd Street in Manhattan, Curtis issued *Target Comics* and *Blue Bolt*. The former featured Carl Burgos's the White Streak, Basil Wolverton's eccentric Spacehawk, and Bob Wood's the Target. The hero

of the second title was Blue Bolt, a character that represented the first collaboration of the formidable team of Joe Simon and Jack Kirby.

Also available on newsstands in the early 1940s were Nita Publications's *Whirlwind Comics* (with Cyclone), Bilbara Publishing's *Cyclone Comics* (featuring Tornado Tom), Lev Gleason's *Silver Streak* (starring the title character and the villainous Claw), Holyoke's *Cat-Man*, Hyper's *Hyper Mystery* (starring Hyper the Phenomenal), and dozens more.

Inevitably, the novelty value of costumed superheroes faded, and the genre became ripe for parody. The comic book industry produced a number of mock heroes in the early 1940s, including Sparky Watts, A1 T. Tude, Stuporman, and

Powerhouse Pepper. By far the best—and most insightful—sendup of the superhero genre was Street & Smith's *Supersnipe Comics*. Written by Ed Gruskin, the feature had trial runs in *Shadow Comics* and *Doc Savage Comics* before graduating to a bimonthly title of its own in the fall of 1942. The charming central character was Koppy McFad, also known as "The Boy with the Most Comic Books in America." An imaginative, well-meaning lad, Koppy was driven by dreams of glory that were fueled by the enormous quantities of comic books he read. Above all else, he longed to be a superhero. Undaunted by reality, Koppy put together a costume from his grandfather's red flannels, his father's lodge cape, and his own tennis shoes. Thus attired, he set out to fight crime as Supersnipe. Koppy's heroic alter-ego had no super strength, however, and couldn't fly, either, so he got around mainly on foot or by bicycle.

Now and then Koppy would have dream-sequence adventures in which Supersnipe was a real, grown-up superman, complete with rippling muscles, skin-tight costume, and flowing cape. Curiously, though, Supersnipe's head remained that of a small boy. George Marcoux, who had assisted on the *Skippy* newspaper strip and drawn a kid strip of his own, *Toddy*, was the artist for Koppy's real-life adventures. The amusing dream sequences were

illustrated by another newspaper veteran, C. M. Payne.

Supersnipe was refreshing because it poked fun at the whole idea of costumed heroes and youthful aspirations to adventure. Often, the situations that Koppy perceived to be dire crimes turned out to be far less sinister, and when he did encounter crooks, they were petty small-timers who were far removed from the evil masterminds of the boy's imagination. Most of the stories had a pleasant undertone of the sort of smalltown-America humor that typified radio shows like *Fibber McGee and Molly* and *The Great Gildersleeve*. *Supersnipe* enjoyed a respectable forty-four-issue run that concluded in 1949.

The success of *Supersnipe* proved that readers were willing to laugh at superheroes but, by the middle 1940s, the even greater success of many of the "straight" superheroes meant that the comic book industry was enjoying its best years to date. For example, in 1944 DC was publishing nineteen different titles and running up combined monthly sales of over 8,500,000 copies. In 1945 Fawcett, with eight titles, reported sales of nearly 4,500,000 each month. Their *Captain Marvel Adventures* alone averaged over 1,300,000 copies per issue. That same year MLJ's five titles had

combined sales of nearly 2,000,000 monthly, Quality's nine titles sold over 1,500,000, and the American Comics Group's (ACG) two funny animal books, *Giggle Comics* and *Ha Ha Comics*, sold over 650,000 combined.

A publisher usually made six cents on every ten-cent comic book sold. On a book such as *Captain Marvel*, Fawcett would take in about $78,000 per issue for a total of around $936,000 a year. DC's gross for 1945, when they'd increased their roster to twenty-one titles, was in the neighborhood of $6,500,000, and that doesn't include profits from toys, movies, radio shows, and other forms of licensing and merchandising. Even ACG, with only *Giggle* and *Ha Ha* at that point, could count on an annual gross take of almost $500,000. Sales figures like these are what inspired the continuing expansion of the comic book industry during the war years and after.

Writer Ed Gruskin created Supersnipe, the musclebound alter ego of comic book collector Koppy McFad. The coer of *Supersnipe* #13, drawn by George Marcoux, depicts one of Koppy's dreams of glory.

©1944 by Street & Smith Publications

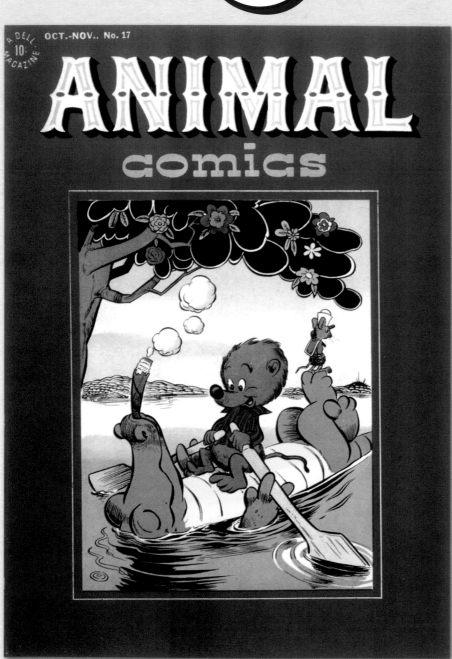

OCT.-NOV.. No. 17

A DELL 10¢ MAGAZINE

ANIMAL comics

Superheroes weren't the only game in town in the 1930s and '40s. "Funny animal" comics thrived and delighted millions of readers. One of these titles was *Animal Comics*, the first home of Walt Kelly's great character Pogo. Kelly's mastery of brushwork and design shows on this 1945 cover.

©1945 by Oskar Lebeck

In the 1930s and 1940s there was a good deal more to be found in comic books than just superheroes and costumed crimefighters. During those years, when the comic book market was still expanding, quite a few comic books really were comic. All sorts of funny stuff was available, from relatively sophisticated satire to knockabout burlesque to the kind of bunny-rabbit whimsy that produced giggles in the nursery. The decade of the forties, especially, was a period when publishers sought to expand their audience in both directions, luring older readers with such things as true crime and sexy women and enticing younger readers with more wholesome fare. Most of the titles aimed at tots were humorous, and a great many of them featured funny animals.

The king of the animals since the late 1920s was Walt Disney, and his screen characters had begun appearing on newsstands in the middle 1930s. *Mickey Mouse Magazine* was issued in the summer of 1935 by K.K. Publications. This company represented a partnership between the Whitman Publishing Company and Disney's Kay Kamen. A former Kansas City department store executive and advertising man, Kamen had been hired by the Disney studio in 1932 to set up a New York-based merchandising department and handle the licensing of the Disney cartoon animals. It was during Kamen's early years with the organization that the Walt Disney name and familiar stylized signature began showing up on products that bore the likenesses of Mickey, Donald Duck, and the rest of the cartoon family. This merchandising provided a visual link between Walt Disney himself and the characters his company controlled. It also helped to make Disney one of the best-known men in America.

Mickey Mouse Magazine was not exactly a true comic book. With the debut issue measuring 10¼ by 13¼ inches, it was slightly larger than what would later become the industry standard. With the second issue, dimensions were trimmed to 8½ by 11½, and a heavier paper stock was used. In the early issues readers got no more than four pages of comics; the rest of each issue consisted of text stories about Mickey, fairy tales, poems, puzzles, a "Wise Quacks" joke page edited by Donald Duck, and sundry other features and fillers. Oskar Lebeck contributed an assortment of original strips and stories, most notably a feature starring Peter the Farm Detective. By 1940 five pages of reprints, including the *Mickey Mouse* daily and, usually, a *Donald Duck* Sunday page were highlights of each issue.

Walt Disney's Comics & Stories replaced Mickey's mag in the fall of 1940, with Dell now joining in as

publisher. The new book was originally made up almost entirely of newspaper reprints—Floyd Gottfredson's splendid mock-adventure *Mickey* dailies, A1 Taliafero's funny gag-a-day *Donald Duck* strips, and various Sundays, including the *Silly Symphony* pages. A change was made in 1943 when the magazine's leadoff stories became original Donald Duck adventures. The artist and writer was an ex-gag cartoonist and animator named Carl Barks (see sidebar), whose energetic drawing style and whimsical, imaginative stories won him two generations of loyal fans.

The Disney stable proved to be a gold mine, so Dell went on to license the Warner Brothers animated cartoon characters. The first issue of *Looney Tunes* and *Merrie Melodies* appeared late in 1941 with individual stories devoted to Porky Pig, Elmer Fudd, and Bugs Bunny. In the comic's early days, the artwork was produced on both coasts. Chase Craig (who drew Porky) and Roger Armstrong (Mary Jane and Sniffles) were based in Southern California; George Storm (Bugs Bunny) was in Manhattan. So was a talented cartoonist named Walt Kelly, ▶

Donald Duck gets into the holiday spirit on the cover of *Mickey Mouse Magazine* #52.

©1940 by K. K. Publications, Inc.

Walt Kelly brought his cartoon style to a 1943 *Pat, Patsy and Pete* adventure that appeared in Looney Tunes.

©1943 by R. S. Callender

The cover of *Looney Tunes* #6 bears the signature of cartoon producer Leon Schlesinger, who neither wrote nor drew it.

©1942 by Leon Schlesinger Productions

Carl Barks

Unsung and anonymous during his active years in comic books, Carl Barks is now acclaimed as one of the medium's authentic geniuses. He gained his fame by drawing ducks, but because the ducks were the property of Walt Disney, Barks was never allowed to sign his work. Yet, because of the quality and individuality of what he did, he gradually became one of the most well-known and admired cartoonists in the world.

Carl Barks was born in a remote part of eastern Oregon in 1901, and by the late 1920s had started to sell his cartoon drawings. He avoided the crowded New Yorker-style market by aiming lower, selling gags to *College Humor* and *Judge*. He was even more successful with markets that were receptive to mildly risque material. Gags of this sort, which Barks built around well-endowed ladies in various states of undress, were especially well received by a Minneapolis-based magazine called *The Calgary Eye-Opener*. Barks accepted a staff job there in 1931 and stayed with the magazine until 1935, when he got a job with the Walt Disney studios in Los Angeles.

Although hired for twenty dollars a week as an animated cartoon "in-betweener" (an artist who creates the drawings that fill in the movement between key drawings made by more experienced animators), Barks quickly displayed an inventiveness that convinced the studio he was better suited to the story department. He remained there until the early 1940s, when he decided to quit Disney and try his hand at something else.

"Something else" turned out to be comic books. Before leaving Disney, Barks (along with artist Jack Hannah) had worked on a one-shot 1942 comic called *Donald Duck Finds Pirate Gold*, written by Bob Karp. Based on a never-produced animated cartoon, it was the first original Donald Duck comic book. Late in 1942 Barks heard that Dell-Western wanted somebody to do original ten-page stories to be added to the lineup of *Walt Disney's Comics & Stories*. He was hired and his first work appeared in issue #31 (April 1943).

Soon after, Barks was writing as well as drawing. His most notable innovation was to broaden Donald Duck's character. "Instead of making just a quarrelsome little guy out of him, I made a sympathetic character," Barks has recalled. "He was sometimes a villain, and he was often a real good guy and at all times he was just a blundering person like the average human being."

Donald's three nephews—Huey, Dewey, and Louie—underwent changes, too, becoming resourceful and inventive. "I broadened them like I did Donald, started out with mischievous little guys and ended up with little scientists, you might say."

Barks added full-length Donald books to his schedule in 1943. It was with the stories produced from this point onward—"The Mummy's Ring," "Frozen Gold," "Volcano Valley"— that Barks hit his stride. With plenty of space to move around in, he created carefully plotted graphic novels. The stories were full of adventure, action, comedy, and satire. They were set in exotic locales and featured some of the best cartooning and visual storytelling ever to be found in comic books.

A 1947 adventure called "Christmas on Bear Mountain" introduced Barks's major creation —Uncle Scrooge. Penurious, paranoid about protecting his vast fortune from the scheming Beagle Boys and other menaces, yet gruffly fond of Donald and the nephews, Uncle Scrooge is at once whimsical and delightfully real. Other characters that Barks vividly brought to life include inventor Gyro Gearloose and the supremely insincere Gladstone Gander.

Barks retired at the age of 65 and has devoted himself since to painting. These works, many of which feature, yes, ducks, are eagerly sought by collectors. His comic book work has been continually reprinted and, since Walt Disney's death in 1966, Barks's important contribution to the Disney family has been publicly acknowledged by comic book publishers and by the Disney organization.

Barks's Donald Duck and Uncle Scrooge adventures are models of effective plotting, characterization, and visual storytelling.

who'd returned to the East after toiling in the Disney studios as an animator. In time, he'd find international fame as the creator of the *Pogo* newspaper strip, but his early work was more modest. His first feature for *Looney Tunes* was *Kandi the Cave Kid* and it was credited, as were all the stories in each issue, to Leon Schlesinger, the non-drawing (and, by all accounts, generally uncreative) producer of the Warner movie cartoons.

Win Smith, a former Disney employee who'd done early artwork on the *Mickey Mouse* daily, drew the very first *Bugs Bunny* story before Storm tried his hand for a few issues. *Looney Tunes* also gave space to an alternating variety of other characters, such as Chester Turtle, Ringy Roonga, and Charlie Carrot, one of the few vegetables ever to appear in a comic book feature of his own; logically enough, Charlie's girlfriend was a tomato. *Pat, Patsy and Pete*, about two kids and a talking penguin, was not a Warner property, but it ran in the magazine for several years. Smith started the feature and eventually handed it to Storm. Kelly drew six episodes in 1943, converting it into a raucous slapstick comedy.

Andy Panda, a product of the Walter Lantz animation studios, wound up in *The Funnies* #61 (October 1941) when the magazine was still playing it straight; Andy's earliest coworkers were Captain Midnight, Phantasmo, and Philo Vance.

With the sixty-fifth issue July 1942) the book's title was changed to *New Funnies* and offered a potpourri of Lantz characters and comedy and fantasy characters from other sources. Lantz was represented by *Andy, Oswald the Rabbit, Li'l Eightball*, and his most popular and enduring creation, *Woody Woodpecker*. From the estate of onetime political cartoonist Johnny Gruelle came *Raggedy Ann* and *Mr. Twee Deedle*. For good measure there were reprints of *Felix the Cat* and the *Peter Rabbit* Sunday page, plus *Billy and Bonny Bee* by Frank Thomas and an updated version of the venerable *Brownies*.

The Whitman-Dell coalition continued its assault on the kid market with the bimonthly *Animal Comics*, which commenced late in 1941. It was here that Walt Kelly's Pogo began his long and successful career. Although the original star of the magazine, from the second issue on, was meant to be Howard Garis's venerable rabbit gentleman Uncle Wiggily, Pogo and his swamp-dwelling pals eventually pushed Unc into a secondary position. The first all-Pogo comic book came along in the spring of

Cartoon producer Walter Lantz never achieved the level of fame of rival Walt Disney, but two of his creations, Andy Panda and Woody Woodpecker, have stayed popular through the decades. This is the cover of *New Funnies* #171.

©1951 by Walter Lantz Productions

Krazy Komics was Marvel's first funny animal title. On the cover of issue #9, Ziggy Pig and Silly Seal indulge in a little wartime propaganda at the expense of Toughy Tomcat.

©1943 by Jest Publishing

Animator Paul Terry's most enduring creation is Mighty Mouse, here on the cover of *Terry-Toons* #49.

©1946 by Timely Comics, Inc.

1946, under the title *Albert the Alligator & Pogo Possum*. By 1949 a *Pogo Possum* magazine was being issued on a fairly regular basis. Finally, in 1949, the *Pogo* newspaper strip started running nationally, and Kelly gained his widest and most enthusiastic audience.

Dell's *Our Gang Comics* and *Raggedy Ann* and Andy, and Western's *Fairy Tale Parade* all arrived in 1942, offering a mixed bag of animal and human characters. In Our Gang Kelly drew the adventures of the kids featured in the MGM comedy shorts, blending melodrama and slapstick far more agreeably than in the shorts themselves. The film series, produced with care by the Hal Roach studio beginning in 1922, had shifted to MGM in the late thirties and was on its last legs by the time Kelly was given the comic book assignment. His success with the feature is a splendid example of the power of his imagination and sense of whimsy.

More Kelly was on view in *Fairy Tale Parade*, in which the artist would typically draw about half of each issue. In addition, he contributed to *Santa Claus Funnies* and *Easter with Mother Goose*, both irregularly issued titles.

Also adapted from MGM properties were Tom & Jerry, Benny Burro, and Barney Bear. Carl Barks eventually took over Benny and, later, the burro teamed up with the bear. These stories were milder and more innocuous than those

Barks was creating for the Disney ducks.

In addition to Ann and Andy stories by veteran artist George Kerr, the *Raggedy Ann* magazine offered *Billy and Bonny Bee* and *Egbert the Elephant*. Most issues of the above-mentioned titles were edited by Oskar Lebeck.

Marvel's earliest funny animal title was *Krazy Komics*, first published in the summer of 1942. Editor Vince Fago and a staff that included Kim Piatt, George Klein, Dave Gantz, and Stan Lee offered an all-new crew of animated cartoon-type characters. Even at this early date, the funny animal formula was looking a bit threadbare, and there were no surprises in such characters as Posty Pelican, Toughy Tomcat & Chester Chipmunk, and A1 Jaffee's Silly Seal & Ziggy Pig. *Krazy's* most unusual feature was an oddity called *The Creeper & Homer*, starring a mysterious villain and a not-too-bright rabbit. It managed now and then to work most of the magazine's artists and writers into the stories and on one occasion publisher Martin Goodman himself appeared to complain, "Ah, woe is me! Krazy Komics is 14 months late, and my laundry hasn't come back from [writer] Stan Lee's." Later in the year, Marvel's *Terry Toons*, adapted from Paul Terry's rather dull movie cartoons, provided a home for Gandy Goose, Oscar Pig, Dinky Duck and, in 1945, Terry's biggest star, Mighty Mouse.

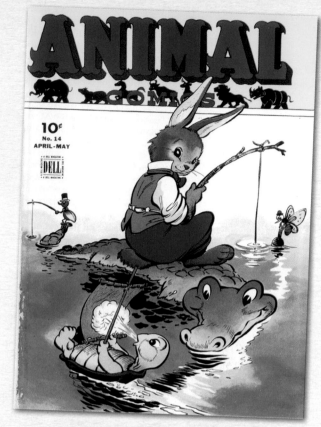

Uncle Wiggily and Albert the Alligator go fishing on the cover of *Animal Comics* #14, drawn by Walt Kelly.

Originally Fawcett announced that its entry in the animated-character derby would be called *Animal Funny Stories*, but when the magazine finally appeared toward the end of 1942 the title was livelier: *Fawcett's Funny Animals*. This being Fawcett's first venture away from straight heroes, the company went to someone with experience in the animated cartoon field to help produce the new comic book. Chicago-born Chad Grothkopf was in his late twenties at the time and had worked in California for Disney. Grothkopf had come east in

1938, when NBC had asked him to work on the very first animated show for the network's fledgling television operation. "There were only fifty sets in the area," he's recalled, "and we'd call up people and tell them we were going on the air. We'd stay on until we ran out of film." To supplement his income, Grothkopf started working in comic books, initially on adventure features like DC's *Sandman and Radio Squad*.

In 1942 Roscoe Fawcett, knowing of Grothkopf's animation background, called him and asked, "Can you make a book for us?" The artist sat down with editorial

director Ralph Daigh and worked out a batch of characters. These included Sherlock Monk, Billy the Kid—a goat cowboy—and Willie the Worm. This last character had originally been created by Grothkopf for NBC television animation. The new book's leading character was to be yet another member of the Marvel family, Hoppy the Marvel Bunny. Like Captain Marvel, he just had to shout, "Shazam!" in order to turn into a red-clad superhero— albeit a long-eared one. The Captain himself appeared on the cover of the first issue of *Fawcett's Funny Animals*, along with Hoppy and the rest of the animal gang.

Grothkopf had a distinctive, appealing style in the animated cartoon tradition. He's said that he enjoyed complete freedom at Fawcett and that the publishers gave him no trouble. He worked with a freelance staff of five or six in a studio on 20th Street in Manhattan, "catty-corner from [drummer] Gene Krupa's." While he was working on Hoppy and his friends, "I had the most fun I ever had in my life."

The All-American branch of DC Comics, under the editorship of Sheldon Mayer, produced DC's first funny animal title. This was *Funny Stuff*, a quarterly that appeared in the summer of 1944. Mayer himself drew J. Rufus Lion, an animal-kingdom version of newspaper-strip star Major Hoople. Blackie Bear, the Three Mouseketeers, and Bulldog

The Fox and the Crow, inevitably headed for conflict, in a story from *Comic Cavalcade* #52. Art is by James F. Davis.

Drumhead were also in the troupe. One of the most interesting characters was McSnurtle the Turtle, alias the Terrific Whatzit. McSnurtle was a parody of DC's superhero-speedster, the Flash, and even wore a miniature Flash costume, winged helmet and all. Martin Naydell, who drew McSnurtle, was also one of the artists on the real Flash at the time.

The benchmark issue of *Funny Stuff* was #5. That one Mayer drew entirely by

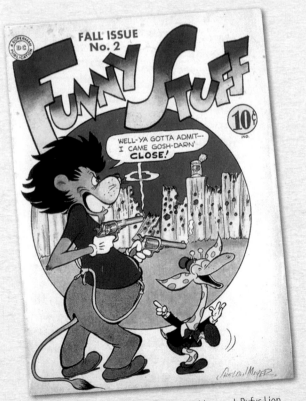

Funny Stuff #2 featured Sheldon Mayer's blustery J. Rufus Lion.

himself, cover and interior. "I had such a yen to sit down and draw pictures again," he explained to readers, "that I drew this whole issue before I could get it out of my system." It was a noble, and funny, effort.

DC turned to movie cartoon characters in 1945 with *Real Screen Comics*. This starred the *Fox and Crow*, a team that had been appearing in a series of animated shorts released by Columbia Pictures. The Fox was a perennial patsy, the Crow the eternal con man who foiled, flimflammed, hoodwinked, and otherwise took advantage of his hapless companion. "[Editor] Whit Ellsworth came out looking for a cartoon subject," animator James F. Davis has explained. "The only thing available was Columbia."

Davis, in addition to working as an animator, was heading up the West Coast branch of the Manhattan-based Ben Sangor shop. Sangor was in partnership with Fred Iger; the pair eventually called themselves the American Comics Group (ACG) and published many successful titles of their own, but the shop also turned out artwork and packaged comics for other publishers. The Sangor specialty was funny animals and, in Hollywood, Davis took over the drawing of the *Fox and Crow* in 1948 and rode herd over a bunch of moonlighting animators and writers. "Well, there were 65 of us

working on those things at one time," he once told an interviewer, "and we used to send back sheets of Strathmore two feet high every month." Eventually DC added *Funny Folks* and other animal titles, and converted hero books like *Comic Cavalcade* and *Leading Comics* to funny stuff; the revamped *Leading Comics* featured a character with the spiffy name of Peter Porkchops.

The Sangor shop also provided the contents for the Pines line of animated comics— *Barnyard*, *Happy*, *Goofy*, and *Coo Coo*. The last title featured Supermouse, whose "great powers, you know, stem from his SUPERCHEESE." This super rodent, created and drawn initially by Kim Platt, appeared on the scene in the autumn of 1942 and was the first animal character to burlesque the more serious human superheroes. Fawcett's Hoppy followed a couple of months later and early in 1943 Marvel made Super Rabbit the star of *Comedy Comics*. Super Rabbit appeared in several short-lived titles, including *Comic Capers* and *All Surprise*, before getting a book of his own in 1944. MLJ's entrant was Super Duck, also known as the Cockeyed Wonder, who waddled into view in the summer of 1943 in *Jolly Jingles*. The MLJ folks lost interest in supermen much earlier than any of their competitors and were retooling for humor far ahead of the rest; until the Duck's debut *Jolly Jingles* had been

known as *Jackpot Comics* and was home to no-nonsense characters like Steel Sterling and the Black Hood.

Giggle Comics, published by ACG as a companion to *Ha Ha Comics*, introduced Superkatt in the spring of 1944. Contrary to his name, the well-meaning feline had no exceptional powers at all. He didn't look particularly heroic, either, since his costume consisted of a baby bonnet, a large bow tie, and a diaper. Dan Gordon, a former animator working in Manhattan, drew Superkatt's adventures; a prolific editor-writer named Richard Hughes provided the scripts. ►

Superkat receives a seasonal surprise on this 1947 *Giggle Comics* cover drawn by Dan Gordon.

Basil Wolverton

Powerhouse Pepper has girl trouble in these panels from "The Face from Space," written and drawn by Basil Wolverton probably in the early 1940s. Wolverton's fondness for rhyme and alliteration was undeniable.

©1971 by Marvel Comics

Basil Wolverton was perhaps the most eccentric cartoonist America ever produced, a master of fine-line detail who had a penchant for the bizarre and the hilariously grotesque. He came to national attention in 1946 after winning *Life* magazine's "Ugliest Girl in the World" art competition. This was a highly publicized "search" for Lena the Hyena, a character who had been featured but never completely revealed in Al Capp's satiric comic strip, *Li'l Abner*. Wolverton's winning interpretation of Lena, complete with hideously protruding teeth, rotted gums, and pocked skin, amused the nation and marked him as a unique talent. His comic book work, much of which pre-dates Lena, showed him to be as adept at grim horror and science-fiction as with wild humor. He worked occasionally for *Mad* and even created powerful, often apocalyptic illustrations for religious publications.

Although Wolverton's *Powerhouse Pepper* owed something to such newspaper strips as *Smokey Stover* and to movies like Olsen and Johnson's *Hellzapoppin*, it was still ninety-nine percent pure Wolverton—lowbrow yet strangely brilliant, inventive and audacious, very much in tune with the baggy-pants burlesque comedy that flourished during World War II.

THE BRAIN-BATS OF VENUS

THERE ARE SOME PLANETS ON WHICH MAN SHOULD NEVER SET FOOT! TWO EARTHMEN FOUND THAT OUT --- TOO LATE!

Wolverton made his name with humorous drawings, but his dramatic cartooning is equally memorable. This bizarre science fiction story originally appeared in *Mr. Mystery* #7 in 1952.

One of Wolverton's favorite devices was alliteration, and before *Powerhouse* was many issues old the artist-writer had given way to his compulsive fascination to such a degree that he could no longer sign his name straight; stories were credited to Basil Weirdwit Wolverton, Basil Bleakbrain Wolverton, Basil Baboonbrain Wolverton, and innumerable variations.

Wolverton was equally fond of internal rhyme. His dialogue, as well as numerous signs and posters that cluttered almost every inch of wall space (and often the floors and ceilings, too) were full of the stuff. A lout about to drop a safe out of a window onto Powerhouse's dome would exclaim "Ah! This is gonna give that little dolt a terrific jolt!" After being insulted, a typical Powerhouse response would go, "That remark makes me sore, bore, and when I get sore, there's war!" Ending up in Egypt in one episode (sign in the sand: Will Sara wear a Sahara tiara?), Powerhouse encounters a reanimated mummy and escorts him back to America. After viewing the joys of modern civilization (which includes a visit to a restaurant named simply Crude Food, wherein are offered such delicacies as blue blackbirds broiled in brown bovine butter and buzz bugs basted in bilge water), the mummy decides he'd be better off in his sarcophagus.

Wolverton's backgrounds were as lively as the foregrounds. He had a fondness for advertisements for dreadful-sounding products and services —"Head hurt? Hog a heap of Hank's Headache Hominy!" "Troubled with a tired, tilted torso? Try tying a timber to your trunk!" "Blue? Blow out your brains with a Bloop and Blinch Brand Blunder-buss!" So it went in the Weirdwit World of Wolverton.

No magazine spoofed *Life* the way *Mad* did, and no one drew women with quite the same . . . level of detail as Basil Wolverton.

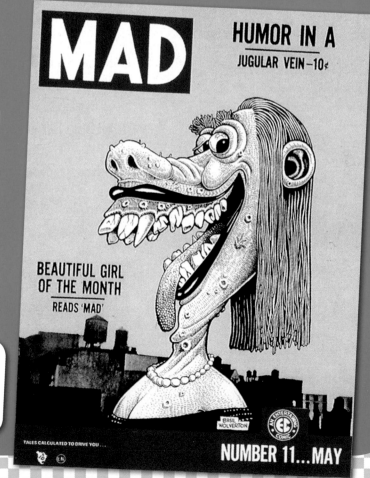

MAD

HUMOR IN A JUGULAR VEIN—10¢

BEAUTIFUL GIRL OF THE MONTH READS 'MAD'

TALES CALCULATED TO DRIVE YOU . . .

NUMBER 11...MAY

Funny animals weren't necessarily the only way to mine laughs. Marvel tried humor with (more or less) human characters in 1942 when it launched *Joker Comics*—modestly billed as "Loaded with Laffs." Headlining *Joker* was Basil Wolverton's Powerhouse Pepper (see sidebar), the only bald superhero of his day. Besides being hairless, Powerhouse didn't need a superman suit to combat evil. Instead, he wore a striped turtleneck sweater, slacks, and heavy work shoes. At last, a hero for the common man! The character's success won him his own comic, as a one-shot in 1943, and as a regular (though shortlived) series five years later.

Powerhouse Pepper was joined in *Joker* by A1 Jaffee's *Squat Car Squad*, a screwball police strip; *Snoop and Dr. Nutzy*, a detective burlesque; *Tessie the Typist*, a working-girl saga; and an assortment of other funny fillers.

DC brought out its first all-funny title in 1943 and called it, logically enough, *All Funny Comics*. A quarterly, it boasted that its sixty-four pages contained "12 Big Laugh Features!" Some of the characters, such as the impecunious private eye Penniless Palmer and the costumed human encyclopedia Genius Jones, had been borrowed from other DC titles. New characters included Two- Gun Percy, Hamilton & Egbert, and Buzzy. Several of the cartoonists recruited for this humor project were newspaper and magazine veterans, some of whom had been turning out funny stuff since before the first world war. These veteran contributors included Tom McNamara, Jack Farr, Jack Callahan, Jimmy Thompson, Paul Fung, and George Storm.

Ray McGill produced *All Funny's Hayfoot Henry*, one of the few cops and robbers features ever written in verse— "I'll take it home and check it for prints. Maybe it'll give me a couple of hints." Well, no one ever claimed it was great verse. Paul Fung contributed *Hamilton & Egbert* and an occasional *Penniless Palmer*. He'd assisted Billy DeBeck on the *Barney Google* newspaper strip and drawn such forgotten strips of his own as *Gus & Gussie* and *Dumb Dora*. The younger *All Funny* contributors included Bernard Baily, original artist on *Two-Gun Percy*, Henry Boltinoff, who drew the cases of a team of dimwitted detectives named Dover & Clover; and Stan Kaye, illustrator of the mock adventures of Genius Jones.

Early in 1942 Famous Funnies Inc. introduced *Jingle Jangle Comics*, a kid-oriented title that provided a mix of human and funny animal features. Steve Douglas was the editor and George Carlson the star cartoonist. A veteran children's book illustrator and puzzlemaker, Carlson was in his middle fifties by the time he ventured into comic books. He'd had a varied career that included painting the dust jacket for Margaret Mitchell's *Gone With the Wind* and ghosting the *Reg'lar Fellers* newspaper strip for credited artist Gene Byrnes. Carlson had been kicking the *Jingle Jangle Tales* idea around for several years (the "Jingle Jangle" title was his creation), and had already tried it as a children's book and, unsuccessfully, as a newspaper Sunday page. Each issue of *Jingle Jangle* contained two of his features—*Jingle Jangle Tales* and The Pie-Face Prince. ▸

The Pie-Face Prince takes possession of a Dingabus in a 1942 *Jingle Jangles* story written and illustrated by George Carlson.

OH, DOCTOR KILDEAR, THAT'LL BE WONDERFUL GOING TO A COSTUME BALL WITH YOU BUT WHAT SHOULD I WEAR?

Leggy, sweet, and a slave to fashion—that was Katy Keene, "America's Pin-Up Queen." Art is by Katy's creator, Bill Woggon.

©1984 by Close-Up, Inc.

Most comic book fans agree that Katy Keene epitomized four-color glamour and wholesome sex appeal. Although the largest part of her audience was composed of teens and pre-teens, Katy wasn't a teenager herself. She was a full-grown young woman who worked initially as a model and later as a Hollywood starlet.

Apparently just about every girl in America goes through a phase where she wants to be a model and/or fashion designer. Katy, whose life was given over chiefly to modeling, posing, and dating, had immediate appeal for an audience that had been unmoved by superheroes, cowboys, or funny animals. Added reader involvement was ensured by Katy's mischievous little sister, Sis, a pig-tailed mischief maker who acted as Katy's accomplice, conscience, and cheerleader. Katy's boyfriends included boxer K.O. Kelly, millionaire playboy Randy Von Ronson, and movie idol Erroll Swoon.

Especially important to Katy's success was the way the feature encouraged reader participation—youngsters were invited to send in designs for Katy's outfits. These designs, rendered by artist Bill Woggon and other staffers, credited each contributor by name and hometown. As cartoonist and longtime Katy fan Trina Robbins has pointed out, "Each episode featured countless costume changes, with every outfit designed by a different reader."

Bill Woggon, who had assisted his brother Elmer on the *Big Chief Wahoo* newspaper strip, created Katy in 1945. The big-eyed beauty made her debut in MLJ's *Wilbur* #5, as a backup feature. Her appeal soon became apparent and she was added to the lineups of *Laugh*, *Pep*, and *Suzie*. In 1949, Katy got a magazine of her own. The book appeared just once that year, once in 1950, and twice in 1951. *Katy Keene* became a quarterly in 1952 and went bimonthly a year later. Nineteen fifty-five brought two new titles, *Katy Keene Fashion Book Magazine* and a 25-cent comic, *Katy Keene Pin-up Parade*.

Woggon, who drew in a simple and direct cartoon style, has said that he was influenced by comic strips like *Fritzi Ritz*, *Brenda Starr*, and *Tillie the Toiler*. The work of George Petty, the airbrush artist who painted pin-ups for *Esquire* magazine, was another influence. [The] Petty Girl was indeed my favorite," Woggon has said, "and inspired me to create . . . Katy Keene." Significantly, each of the three comic strips cited by Woggon occasionally included paper dolls, and would give credit to readers who submitted fashion designs.

Woggon employed several assistants over the years, including Hazel Marten, Cassie Bill, Floyd Norman, Bob MacLeod, Tom Cooke, and Bill Ziegler. Katy's career ended in 1961, but she made a modestly successful comeback in 1983.

The Pie-Face Prince's encounter with the Dingabus continues in a misadventure rife with whimsy by artist and writer George Carlson.

©1942 by Eastern Color Printing Co.

Carlson was a one-man band of a cartoonist who did scripting, pencilling, inking—the works. Apparently dedicated to these stories, Carlson always submitted a one-page synopsis of each one to Steve Douglas. After getting an okay, he would prepare a detailed outline that mixed typed copy and handsome full-color pencil sketches. For his conscientious dedication, Carlson eventually earned twenty-five dollars per page for the twelve pages of material he turned out for each issue. The tales mixed burlesque, fantasy, and word play with his own, individualistic brand of nonsense.

Carlson brought a sophisticated approach to fairy tales, turning out multileveled material in which the visual and verbal elements worked together. The dialogue in his work demonstrated his fascination with language: it contained left-handed puns, and stock phrases twisted into new and unexpected shapes. Quite obviously he was amusing himself first and foremost. And, like Walt Kelly, he had in mind not only the kids who were buying the funny books but the grown-ups who were going to be cajoled into reading the stories aloud.

Among the characters who did turns in Carlson's *Jingle Jangle Tales* were the Youthful Yodeler, who lived on a newly painted mountain and sold all kinds of weather by the yard; the Half-Champion Archer, who wasn't the full-time champ because he never hit the king's special Tuesday target; the Very Horseless Jockey, who became rich from a flavored snowball business and then set out, via steamed-up steam engine, to buy a fine mahogany horse for himself. A delightful variety of unusual props, people, and creatures wandered through Carlson's lively, cluttered pages—a freshly toasted sandwich board, a young idea "with its buttons all neatly sewed on the wrong side," a four-footed yardstick maker, a zigzag zither, a lovely blonde mazurka, and a trio of jellybeans, "all slicked up, with shoe-laces neatly pressed," who go forth into the world to seek their fortune.

Pretzleburg, ruled over by King Hokum without much help from his pie-face offspring Prince Dimwitri, was a place that brought an inspired silliness to the conventions of light opera. The recurrent players were Princess Panetella Murphy, who was more or less the object of Dimwitri's affections and could sometimes be found residing in "her left-footed uncle's second-best castle"; the Raging Raja, billed as the Prince's "favorite enemy"; and the Wicked Green Witch (a longtime resident of Connecticut, Carlson was no doubt inspired here by the common mispronunciation of Greenwich). Prince Dimwitri's interests and adventures were wide-ranging. In one issue he set out to find the coveted Doopsniggle Prize with his cornbeef flavored cabbage plant; in another he went aloft in an eighteen-carat balloon in search of a missing bass drum.

Jingle Jangle certainly appealed to children and probably captivated more than its share of adults, too. But there was another audience that a comic like *Jingle Jangle* could not reach: the teenage audience. Fairly early in the forties comic book publishers discovered that teenagers liked to read about themselves, and that stories about teenagers could be highly salable. Adolescents had only recently been discovered to be a separate tribe. Publishers, film producers, and other entrepreneurs looked at adolescents and saw a large segment of the population whose antics and rituals could be exploited for entertainment purposes and who had money of their own to spend.

College youths inspired popular images in the 1920s, when artist John Held, Jr. and his many imitators started depicting short-skirted flappers and flask-toting "sheiks" in raccoon coats. High school kids, though, didn't really get much public notice until the 1930s,

when swing music and the jitterbug dance craze helped put them on the map. Suddenly, the high-energy antics of high-school boys and girls were noted by newspapers, magazines, and newsreels, which in turn piqued the interest (and sometimes dismay) of grownups. More notably, this rush of attention caught the fancy of younger children, who couldn't wait to be teenagers themselves. So it was that teenagers, adults, and young kids provided a large audience in the late thirties and early forties for teen-based entertainments.

Henry Aldrich, the well-meaning but bumbling teen who was the prime inspiration for most of the early comic book high schoolers, had first appeared in 1938 in Clifford Goldsmith's Broadway play *What a Life*. Henry and his pal Homer soon made the leap to radio and then to the movies. Jackie Cooper was the first screen Henry; Jimmy Lydon, a gawkier, more overtly comic young fellow, took over the role in the early 1940s. Although B-films, the Henry Aldrich pictures were produced by Paramount with a modest gloss, much as MGM brought appealing production values to their own teen comedies—the Andy Hardy series with Mickey Rooney. Preoccupied with girls, cars, and school, Henry and Andy saw no reason why they shouldn't have all the rights and perks of adulthood

—after all, they'd be grown up any day now! But their elaborate schemes and dreams of glory led them into all sorts of unforeseen complications. The boys' parents, of course, rarely understood them. Mothers and fathers tried to be understanding, but often acted as though Henry and Andy had contracted some rare disease that had caused them to run amok.

Parental disquiet aside, the Henry Aldrich and Andy Hardy comedies were very successful, and spurred comic book publishers into offering funny teens of their own. MLJ was the first to be influenced by the newly emergent American teeenager. Beginning in 1941, the company began adding characters to titles that had previously contained nothing but superheroes, masked marvels, and similarly violent vigilante types. MLJ's most ▶

Four Color #447 featuring Andy Hardy appeared in 1953, after the popularity of "traditional" teen comics had faded considerably.

©1952 by Western Printing & Lithographing Co.

John Stanley's Little Lulu

Created by cartoonist Marge Henderson Buell for a series of gag panels that began in The *Saturday Evening Post* in 1935, it is as a comic book character that Little Lulu is most fondly remembered. The clever little girl with the corkscrew curls, bright red dress, and tiny red hat made her comic book debut in Dell's *Four Color* #74 in 1945, and stepped up to a title of her own late in 1947. The long-running comic, though officially titled *Marge's Little Lulu*, was masterminded by artist-writer John Stanley.

What Stanley provided, after having written and drawn the first couple of *Little Lulu* issues by himself, were rough storyboards for artist Irving Tripp to follow. Comics historian Mike Barrier explained, "To say that Stanley 'wrote' *Little Lulu* is actually a little deceptive, since he was responsible for more than the plots and the dialogue. He sketched each story in rough form, so that he controlled the staging within each panel and the appearance and attitudes of the characters." Stanley's penciled pages would be enlarged, inked by Tripp (with occasional assists from Gordon Rose and others), and lettered.

Stanley inherited Lulu's boyfriend/antagonist Tubby from the original gag cartoons (where the fat boy was named Joe), but he invented most of the other characters. These include truant officer Mr. McNabbem, Wilbur Van Snobbe, Witch Hazel & Little Itch, and the bullying West Side Boys. As Mike Barrier has pointed out, Stanley's conception of Lulu is quite different from the bratty kid of the Post era. Eventually, "Lulu . . . became a 'good little girl' who outsmarted the boys instead of triumphing through sheer brass, as she had in the past. Many of the stories built around the [boy vs. girl] rivalry theme are ingenious and funny, and the best of them spiral upward until the boys become the victims of comic catastrophe."

Lulu's adventures were intelligent and refreshingly low key. These attributes, coupled with Stanley's simple storytelling style, entertained a generation of kids and inspired many of them to remain fans into their adult lives.

Stanley worked on *Little Lulu* until 1961; in all, he was responsible for about 150 issues. The comic book continued without him (many post- Stanley issues simply reprint his earlier stories) and was published until 1984. Today, the best of Stanley's Lulu stories are available in quality hardcovers published for the collector market.

successful kid star was Bob Montana's *Archie*, who changed not just the company's fortunes, but its very name, as well.

Archie arrived in *Pep Comics* #22 and *Jackpot Comics* #4, accompanied by his wholesome blonde girlfriend, Betty, and his deceptively dimwitted pal, Jughead. The dark-haired Veronica came slinking into Archie's life a few months later. Montana had an attractive, cartoony style and most of the Archie plots were breezy, formulaic, and spiced with agreeable doses of slapstick.

The Archie version of teen life was one that a great many readers took to and the character's star began to rise.

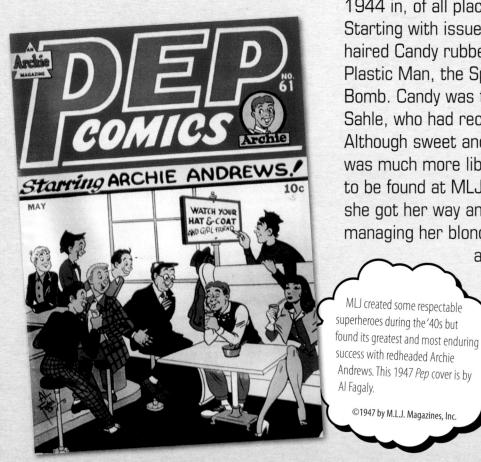

The first issue of Archie's own magazine came out in the fall of 1942 and by late 1947 he'd nudged all the serious heroes out of *Pep*. Bob Montana had left the Archie comic books in the middle forties to take care of the new Archie newspaper strip; artists who carried on in the comic books included Harry Sahle, Bill Vigoda, and Dan DeCarlo. (An ironic side note to the Archie success story is that Archie Comics has made periodic attempts since the 1960s to revive the original MLJ superheroes and to introduce wholly new superhero characters; each attempt has failed.)

The Quality Comics Group's most successful teenager showed up in late 1944 in, of all places, *Police Comics*. Starting with issue #37, sexy, chestnut-haired Candy rubbed shoulders with Plastic Man, the Spirit, and the Human Bomb. Candy was the creation of Harry Sahle, who had recently left Archie. Although sweet and wholesome, Candy was much more liberated than the girls to be found at MLJ. She saw to it that she got her way and was very adept at managing her blond boyfriend, Ted, and her plump businessman father.
Candy was much like the energetic young ladies who were featured in *A Date with Judy*, *Meet Corliss*

Archer, and other established radio shows. (Both Judy and Corliss, by the way, would have comic books of their own later in the forties). Candy won her own comic in the summer of 1947 and enjoyed a run of sixty-four issues. Like all her sisters, she was expert with the latest slang—"But definitely," "I know you're pooched," "all reet," and so forth. She doted on her boyfriends and her collection of jitterbug platters—hobbies that caused her parents no end of consternation.

DC's earliest entry in the teen sweepstakes was also a jive cat, but nowhere near as hep as Candy. His name was *Buzzy* and he came along late in 1943 in All Funny. Not only did he collect phonograph records, he played the trumpet, too. His pretty girlfriend, Susie, adored this facet of Buzzy's personality, but her portly businessman father couldn't stand the sound of the kid's bleating horn. Just a few toots and the old guy would boot Buzzy from the house and attempt mayhem on the boy's scrawny body—a frenzied reaction that caused Susie to frequently exclaim, "Popsy is killing Buzzy!" Written and drawn in kinetic style by the admirable George Storm, the feature had a certain wacky appeal. Buzzy, however, wasn't exactly a reasonable facsimile of a 1940s adolescent. He seemed stiff in his suit and tie and the junky, slogan-covered jalopy he drove looked like something that might have been driven a decade earlier by newspaper-strip star Harold Teen. Even so, Buzzy graduated to a magazine of his own by 1944, and although Storm abandoned his offspring not long after, Buzzy hung on until 1958.

The American Comics Group brought added slapstick to the teen formula with Cookie, a diminutive, wide-eyed kid who first surfaced in *Topsy-Turvy Comics*, a one-shot that came out in the spring of 1945. Exactly a year later he returned in his own bimonthly. Cookie may not have been as tall as his fellow teen stars, but he did have the requisite supporting cast— irascible businessman father, understanding mother, beautiful blonde girlfriend (named Angelpuss, no less), slangspewing pal (named Jitterbuck), and a tall, conniving rival (named Zoot). What made Cookie stand out from Buzzy and all the rest was that he was drawn by Dan Gordon, a former cartoon animator who produced a version of teen life that had the flavor of the eccentric wildness of cartoon director Tex Avery or the Warner Bros. Looney Tunes. Gordon's stories were full of violent pratfalls, lowbrow jokes, and gags involving outrageous props.

Teen titles continued to proliferate into the later 1940s, and were one of the factors that contributed to the (temporary) demise of superheroes. Binky, Kathy, Ozzie, Ginger, Jeanie, Junior, Mitzi, Patsy Walker, Georgie, and dozens of others were to be found on the roster of just about every comic book publisher.

Beyond doubt the most unusual attempt to cash in on the teenage craze was made by ACG in 1947, when it introduced *Hi-Jinx*. "A brand-new idea in comics," the magazine promised the public. "Teenage animal funnies." Even the invitation to "meet some real hepcats," didn't save this one and, despite contributions from Dan Gordon and Milt Gross, the comic expired after just seven issues.

By the end of World War II, the innate innocuousness of teen comics had become apparent to the reading public. Even Dell's *Henry Aldrich* comic, introduced in 1950, could not stop the comic book industry's gravitation to a new, rougher sort of fare that would dominate the first decade of the postwar era.

Against all odds, Susie's dad enjoys the bleat of Buzzy's trumpet. This copy of *Buzzy* #1 was once owned by the feature's artist, George Storm.

©1944 by National Periodical Publications, Inc.

The American Comics Group offered *Hi-Jinx*, a peculiar mix of the teen and funny animal genres.

©1948 by B & I Publishing Co., Inc.

In *Gay Comics* #31, Flicker's in love, but few readers cared by the time this issue appeared in 1948. Another more "serious" sort of comic book had begun to dominate the industry.

©1948 by USA Comic Magazine Corp.

CHAPTER 8

Girls! Romance! Horrors!

FEATURING...

THE VAULT-KEEPER

THE CRYPT-KEEPER

THE OLD WITCH

Horror comics from a multitude of publishers sold in tremendous numbers in the early 1950s. Few titles delivered more effectively than EC Comics's *The Vault of Horror*. Johnny Craig created the crisp artwork for this touch of Christmas cheer with an EC spin.

©1954 by L. L. Publishing Company, Inc.

Overall sales of comic books continued to increase during the middle and late 1940s. In 1945 the combined annual sales of ten of the top publishers amounted to approximately 275,000,000 copies. By 1947 the figure had climbed to 300,000,000 and in 1949 it was nearly 340,000,000. What these fantastic sales figures don't show is the desperation that plagued comic book publishers, and the anxious, industry-wide retooling for new product. The supermen and wonderwomen, in particular, had a difficult time adjusting to the postwar era. America's four years of war had produced an audience that was older and more sophisticated; the caped, long-underwear crowd suddenly seemed passe.

Even though interest in costumed crimefighters was waning, there was still big money to be made in comic book publishing. All that was needed was some rethinking. The audience for comic books had grown impressively throughout the war years, particularly among adults. Most of the millions of new, adult readers were servicemen, whose tastes account for many of the changes that took place in comic books beginning in the middle 1940s. In an effort to appeal to the huge Post Exchange readership, publishers had added more sex, violence, and humor to their comics, and had also introduced new varieties of comics.

Good-looking women were featured on innumerable Fiction House comics. *Planet #44* suggests that even purple aliens with snouts for arms can have an eye for the ladies.

©1946 by Love Romances Pub. Co.

Fiction House loved to combine jungle thrills with half-dressed women. This cover was drawn by Dan Zolnerowich.

©1942 by Glen Ken Pub. Co.

Basic fact: One way to appeal to a young male readership is to offer pictures of young, voluptuous females. In the days when mildly risque "cheesecake" pin-up magazines enjoyed healthy circulations, comic books were one more place to girl watch. The chief source of what dedicated collectors now refer to as "good girl" art in the 1940s was the comics published by the Fiction House company. Good girl art doesn't refer to *Wonder Woman* or to reprints of the *Mary Worth* newspaper strip, but rather to the spicy stories tailored for teenage boys and GIs. Fiction House, the undisputed champ of this sort of material, was headquartered on Eighth Avenue in Manhattan. It turned out a line of comic books with deceptively mild titles—*Planet, Wings, Jungle, Fight, Jumbo*— and fairly steamy contents.

As the names of the magazines suggest, the Fiction House gang was able to introduce sexy ladies into every sort of situation and locale. Fiction House's readers encountered amply constructed and sparsely clad young women on the land, the sea, and in the air. Deep in the jungles, beautiful blondes wore leopard-skin undies, while off on a remote planet a lovely redhead might sport a chrome-plated bra, flimsy skirt, and little else. Although the East Coast street jargon of the time dubbed these magazines "headlight comics," the artists turning out the product were fascinated not only with breasts, but also with buttocks, thighs, and just about any other portion of the female anatomy that could be thrust excitingly against—or through— provocative clothing.

The artists had an easier time than the scriptwriters, who had to continually devise new excuses for introducing nearly naked girls into yarns that allegedly dealt with prizefighting, delivering the airmail, exploring Mars, or fighting the Japanese in the Pacific. Not surprisingly, the writers' ingenuity proved boundless, and the gals showed up in story after story, just like Clockwork.

Fiction House had begun life in the 1920s as a publisher of pulp fiction. Owned by the Two Jacks—Kelly and Glennister—the Fiction House lineup included *Action Stories*, *Wings*, and *Fight Stories*. Publication of all titles was suspended at the end of 1932 but a few years later T. T. Scott, who'd been the company's secretary, revived the Fiction House pulp line and added *Jungle Stories* and *Planet Stories*. Persuaded by the Eisner-Iger shop to go into comic books, Scott introduced his first, *Jumbo Comics*, in the summer of 1938. Most of his later comics were adaptations of the Fiction House pulps. By the early 1940s Eisner was on his own and Iger was heading up the shop, providing the material for all of Scott's comics. Interestingly enough, quite a bit of the shop's good girl art was drawn by women. Lily Renee, Fran Hopper, and Marcia Snyder were all employed by Iger,

The Jerry Iger studio churned out a small mountain of "good girl" art for Fiction House and other publishers. Artist Marcia Snyder worked in the Iger shop and was one of the few women artists in comics. Her *Camilla* page (above) dates from the mid '40s. Lily Renee also worked for Iger—"Lost World" (below) was published by Fiction House in 1945.

©1945 by Fiction House Magazines

and illustrated the adventures of such characters as the jungle girl Camilla, Glory Forbes, and Senorita Rio.

The Fiction House preoccupation with sex became obvious with only a glance at their front covers. Of all the hundreds of gaudy covers that graced the company's comic books throughout the forties, there is hardly a one that doesn't prominently feature a pretty girl somewhere in the action. A typical *Planet Comics* cover, for instance, might depict the Lizard Tyrant of the Twilight Worlds or the Raiders of the Red Moon, but there's also a distressed damsel flashing considerable amounts of flesh in the foreground. The formula was the same with the covers of *Wings Comics*, *Fight Comics*, *Jungle Comics*, and the rest. Readers would enjoy an authentic World War II aircraft, realistically rendered, or believable African flora and fauna, but there also would be a pretty girl with her skirt hiked above her garters and her blouse torn down to her midriff.

Since Fiction House was an equal opportunity employer, a whole flock of female characters starred in features of their own. The resident sexpot in *Fight Comics* for a couple of years was Senorita Rio,

"once in Hollywood, now a U.S. secret agent," who fought Axis spies in South America. Her investigations invariably called for several changes of costume and her faithful readers were allowed to watch every one of them. *Ranger Comics* boasted two female stars. One was Glory Forbes, yet another secret

Sheena debuted in 1938 and got her own book four years later. Her sexy good looks had a huge influence on the look and tone of comic books of the '40s and '50s.

©1942 by Fiction House Magazines

Artist Bob Lubbers demonstrated his skill with "good girl" art on the cover of *Wings* #92.

©1948 by Fiction House Magazines

agent type, and the other was Firehair, a red-haired lass who played Lone Ranger games in the Old West while wearing a short buckskin dress and not much else. The artist who drew more Firehair adventures than anyone else was Bob Lubbers, who later moved on to good girl newspaper strips such as *Long Sam* and *Robin Malone*.

Fiction House offered quite a few other fetching female strips—*Mysta of the Moon*, *Gale Allen and the Girl Squadron*, *Patsy Pinup*, *Sky Girl*, *Futura*, and *Camilla*. Their most successful and best remembered female character was Sheena, Queen of the Jungle, who debuted in *Jumbo Comics* in 1938 and continued in the title (and on nearly every cover) until its final issue, published in 1953. Leggy, buxom, and blonde, Sheena was the quintessential jungle girl. Young female readers may have appreciated her fearlessness against lions, crocodiles, and surly natives, but Sheena's most ardent fans, undoubtedly, were boys and young men. (This fan interest was fervid enough, in fact, to inspire a syndicated *Sheena* television series that aired in 1955, two years after the demise of *Jumbo Comics*; statuesque Irish McCalla starred as the jungle girl.)

Since being a jungle girl afforded obvious opportunities for going around with a minimum of clothing, Fiction House could not resist the temptation to offer another besides Sheena. The company's

variation was Tiger Girl, who turned out to be one of the most successful of the industry's Sheena surrogates. She first appeared in *Fight Comics* #32 (June 1944) and was drawn originally by Matt Baker (see sidebar), one of the stars of the Iger shop and a master of the good girl style. Also known as Princess Vishnu, the blonde Tiger Girl wore a two-piece tigerskin bathing suit, lived in a hidden temple, and served as a guardian of the people and animals who lived in her part of India. Tiger Girl was also very handy with a bullwhip. The character remained in *Fight* until 1952 and appeared, battling a variety of wilderness threats, on every cover from issue #49 through #81.

A modest wave of other new jungle girls came along in the immediate postwar years, many of them in the Pines line of comics. Princess Pantha began in *Exciting Comics* #56 (October 1946) and soon nudged Doc Strange out of the title's star spot. Drawn initially by Ralph Mayo, the feature dealt with "a mere girl" who worked as a big game hunter. The dark-haired Pantha did her hunting clad in a two-piece leopard-skin bathing suit, accompanied by a ►

Fiction House's Sheena, Queen of the Jungle—drawn here by Bob Webb—set the new standard for "ladylike" comic book attire.

©1942 by Real Adventure Publishing Co.

Sheena inspired many leggy imitators. Judy of the Jungle knocked the superhero Black Terror off the cover of Standard's *Exciting Comics*. This cover was drawn by Alex Schomburg, who occasionally signed as "Xela."

©1948 by Better Publications, Inc.

Matt Baker

Matt Baker's lively 1947 drawing of the character Flamingo illustrates his gift for depicting pretty girls.

©1984 by The Caplin-Iger Co., Ltd.

A prolific and very influential comic book artist, Matt Baker enjoyed a flourishing career from the middle 1940s until his death in 1955. One of the few blacks employed in comics in those days, he was a leading creator of what comic book collectors refer to as "good girl" art.

Baker was born around 1918 and went to work for the Iger shop early in 1946. His arrival on the comic book scene coincided with the beginning of the decline of the superhero genre. The companies that tied their futures to pretty-girl comics found Baker's work marketable and highly appealing. Fox and Fiction House, in particular, showcased his art. Baker's pages, filled with his immediately identifiable slim, large-breasted, and long-legged heroines, appeared frequently in titles from both companies.

It was for Fox that Baker drew his most famous character, Phantom Lady. Though that title survived less than two years, the character— busty, athletic, and skimpily costumed— made a lasting impression on readers and collectors. Baker's pin-up- style interpretation of *Phantom Lady* is boyishly enthusiastic, and doubly interesting because of its unabashed bondage elements. These attributes have turned the Fox/Baker Phantom Lady into a valuable collector's title.

Baker also drew material that was more sedate, including the *Classics Illustrated* adaptation of *Lorna Doone* that appeared in issue #32 (December 1946). As comic books turned away from sexy material in the mid-fifties, Baker switched to westerns, war stories, and true crime. In addition, he did particularly fine work for St. John's *Teen-Age Romances* and *Going Steady*, and other romance titles. He even drew three issues of Dell's *Lassie*. According to comic book artist Jay Disbrow's book, *The Iger Comics Kingdom*, Baker died of a "congenital illness" at age 37. Some sources speculate that the culprit was heart failure brought on by overwork.

blond explorer-writer-hunk named Dane Hunter. Equally at home in any of the jungles of the world, Pantha prowled not only in Africa but in Central Asia, Mexico, and New Guinea. After the departure of Ralph Mayo, Pantha's adventures were illustrated by Artie Saaf and Rafael Astarita, who, like Mayo, were alumni of Fiction House. Pines added two more jungle girls in the spring of 1947—Tygra in *Startling Comics* and Judy of the Jungle in *Exciting Comics*.

Never one to miss an exploitable trend, publisher Victor Fox branched out into jungle girls at about the same time as Ned Pines. Rulah, Jungle Princess, who wore a two-piece bathing suit made of what looked to be giraffe skin, took over as leading lady of *All Top Comics* with issue #8, published toward the end of 1947 (the comic had previously been a funny animal book that starred a super feline named Cosmo Cat). Rulah also appeared briefly in *Zoot Comics*. In 1948 Fox introduced Tegra, Jungle Empress, in a magazine of her own. After one issue her name was changed to Zegra and she retired after four more issues. Rulah and Tegra/Zegra were products of the Iger studio.

The jungle genre persevered into the early and middle fifties. Fox was represented during this period by *Jungle Jo* and *Jungle Lil*, both of which began and ended in 1950. Marvel, which called itself Atlas at the time, introduced Lorna

the Jungle Girl in her own magazine in the summer of 1953 and added *Jungle Tales* in 1954. Brunette Jann of the Jungle was sufficiently successful in the latter title that the magazine changed its name to hers with the eighth issue (November 1955). Magazine Enterprises offered a slight variation on the jungle girl theme with Cave Girl in 1953; talented Bob Powell provided the artwork. Fetching though they were, however, none of these characters survived the decade.

Sheena's closest competition as most popular sex object in comic books of the 1940s was a superheroine, Phantom Lady. She'd begun her career, as noted in Chapter 6, in the pages of Quality's *Police Comics* in 1941. Victor Fox got hold of her in 1947 and gave her a magazine of her own. Going out solo changed her somewhat—her costume became even skimpier and her bosom grew impressively larger. She also developed a marked propensity for being tied up and chained, and frequently appeared in these states, especially on the comics' covers. If 1950s cult photo model Betty Page had a fictional predecessor in the bondage stakes, it's Phantom Lady. The art during this kinky heyday was provided by the dependable Matt Baker.

Not every good-girl temptress was a superheroine. Torchy was a sexy, teasing lady who didn't bother with crimefighting

or other strenuous activities—she seemed content merely to display herself. She wore the frilliest black lingerie in the business and first showed up in issue #53 (September 1946) of Quality's *Modern Comics*, home of Blackhawk. She got a magazine of her own three years later. Torchy was

Bill Ward's Torchy was one of the most popular glamor girls in comics. Long-legged and brimming with sex appeal, she was concerned mainly with her wardrobe and boyfriends. The *Modern Comics* panel seen here dates from about 1947.

©Quality Comics Group

SHE'S BEAUTIFUL BUT DUMB THAT'S SUZIE

YOU'LL GET LOADS OF LAUGHS WHEN YOU READ SUZIE COMICS -- AND DON'T FORGET IN SUZIE COMICS YOU'LL ALSO FIND

KATY KEENE SIS GINGER ANGELA FERDIE PUZZLES GAMES STORIES

"Beautiful but dumb"—such was the state of comic book humor in 1949. Suzie was just one of the many pretty girls on MLJ's roster.

©1949 by M.L.J. Magazines, Inc.

created by good girl specialist Bill Ward, whose outrageously sexy men's magazine cartoons would later make him a cult figure. Ward adapted the Torchy character from a strip he'd drawn while in the service; the long-legged blonde's later exploits were rendered by Gill Fox.

Most of the other provocative ladies in the comics of the immediate postwar years were shapely crimefighters like Lady Luck, the Blonde Phantom, and Lee Elias's Black Cat, or they were just plain pretty girls like Suzie, Tessie the Typist, and Millie the Model.

The pretty girl comics maintained their popularity into the early 1950s and helped to supplant the superhero

genre. Unfortunately for the comic book publishers, not everyone liked what the industry was producing. More to the point, sexy women were capable of arousing even more ire and criticism from unsympathetic observers than crimebusting musclemen had ever inspired.

Comics did have a "softer" side at this time—one that demonstrated that if pretty girls meant sex and action, they also meant romance. As the 1940s drew to a close, there was an enormous outpouring of love. It began as a provocative tickle in 1947 and 1948, and then more than a hundred different romance titles hit the stands in 1949,

followed by nearly half a hundred more in 1950. All the major publishers, and quite a few of the minor ones, had gone mushy for dollars. Love was everywhere. Marvel, once the home of heroes, offered about thirty romantic comic books, ranging from *Girl Confessions* to *Romances of the West*. Quality, Fawcett, Lev Gleason, Avon, and DC all joined the love parade. The ever-enterprising Victor Fox was responsible for over two dozen romance comics, seventeen of which contained the word my in the title—*My Desire*, *My Secret*, *My Secret Affair*, *My Great Love*, et al.

Love comics were inspired by confession magazines such as *True Story and True Confessions*, by radio soap operas, and by such increasingly popular newspaper strips as *Mary Worth* and *Rex Morgan*, M.D. In fact, an early precursor of the later wave of love comics was *Romantic Picture Novelettes*, a one-shot (one issue only) issued in 1946 by Vincent Sullivan's Magazine Enterprises. Hiding behind the title were reprints of the *Mary Worth* strip, which revolved around the lovelorn characters encountered by Mary, a kindly, silver-haired lady who was always ready with some good advice. *Mary Worth* and the other soap strips were full of domestic strife, heartache, and, yes, love. "Realistic" in their subject matter, they were drawn in the slickly illustrative Milton Caniff (*Steve Canyon*)

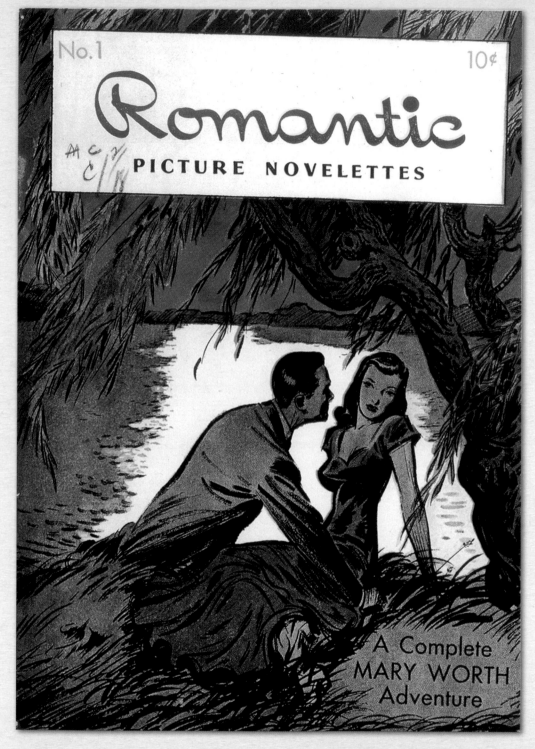

Romantic Picture Novelettes was probably the first romance comic book. Although a one-shot, it encouraged a tidal wave of love comics in the late '40s and early '50s. Mary Worth—the same as the long-running newspaper comic strip—had an eponymous romance comic from 1949-50.

©1946 by Magazine Enterprises, Inc.

manner. All of these elements were adopted by the romance comic books.

The romance comic book format was devised by the team of Simon and Kirby, heretofore noted mainly for their bestselling superheroes (Captain America) and kid gangs (Young Allies). Joe Simon has recalled that he got the love-comic idea while serving in the Coast Guard. "I noticed that there were so many adults, the officers and the men and the people in town, reading kid comic books," he's said. "I felt sure there should be an adult comic book." Intent upon packaging the entire concept, Simon drew sample title pages and a sample cover for his proposed magazine, which he called *Young Romance*, the "Adult Comic Book." When asked why he'd picked the love genre, Simon answered, "It was about the only thing that hadn't been done."

After returning from the service Simon resumed his partnership with Jack Kirby. "[Kirby] loved the idea," Simon recalled. "So we decided, since we weren't working, we would make up the whole book. We spent money on the features, we did part of it and we had [artist] Bill Draut and others doing part of it." As to the scripts—"We wrote the whole thing. We couldn't afford writers."

Simon was surely aware of the soap opera newspaper strips, but he was more influenced by the somewhat darker tone of the confession magazines. The finished package was taken to Maurice Rosenfeld, managing editor of the Prize Group—*Prize Comics*, *Headline*, *Frankenstein*. Rosenfeld and the company's owners, Mike Bleir and Teddy Epstein, were enthusiastic and "we worked out a fifty percent arrangement." Sharing of the profits was unusual at the time and Kirby has said, "We were the first to get percentages."

The first issue of *Young Romance* was published in the fall of 1947 with an impressive S & K cover showing

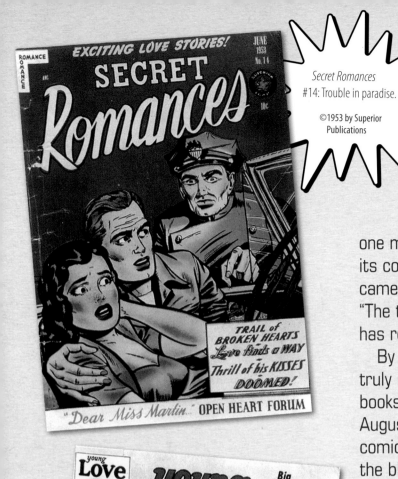

an eternal triangle unfolding in the studio of a handsome young artist. The line "Designed For The More ADULT Readers of Comics" ran beneath the title. The first issue sold out a print run of 500,000 copies. The circulation soon jumped to one million per issue, as did that of its companion title, *Young Love*, which came along at the tail end of 1948. "The things made millions," Simon has recalled.

By the end of the 1940s sales were truly impressive for almost all the love books. According to a report in the August 22, 1949 issue of *Time*, the love comics were "outselling all others, even the blood and thunder variety." Fawcett's *Sweethearts*, for example, was another title that was selling a million copies an issue; the same publisher's *Life Story* accounted for 700,000 copies. Interestingly, the romance comic books were hurting more than just the superhero comics—they also were cutting into the sales of the pulps and the true confession magazines. The venerable *True Story* went so far as to admit that its sales were being hurt by the upstart comics. Not everyone was favorably impressed by the sales power of the

romance comics; *Time* was especially unsympathetic, concluding its love comics piece by asserting, "For pulp magazines the moral was even clearer: no matter how low their standards for fiction, the comics could find lower ones."

Time magazine's criticism of love comics was nothing compared to the firestorm that would be unleashed by another upstart genre: the horror comic. During World War II, Charles Biro's *Crime Does Not Pay* had proved that comic books didn't need heroes in order to sell in big numbers. Meantime, other publishers, notably the Harvey brothers, experimented with more sedate magazines that used no continuing characters. *All-New* and the oddly titled *Hello Pal*, both inaugurated in 1943, featured short stories in comic book form. So did Harvey's *Front Page* in 1945 and *Strange Story* in 1946. These latter titles introduced Bob Powell's Man in Black, who narrated unusual and spooky yarns. By utilizing a sardonic host who would introduce and comment upon the action of the story, Powell was borrowing a device from popular radio shows such as *Inner Sanctum*, *The Whistler*, and *Suspense*. *Suspense*, in fact, used a narrator called the Man in Black during several seasons.

Avon's *Eerie*, the first out-and-out horror comic book, emerged late in 1946. Published as part of the

Adventures Into the *Unknown* was a slick, long-running horror title with familiar themes—like drawings come to life.

©1953 by B & I Publishing Co.

Both *Adventures* covers seen here were drawn by Ogden Whitney.

©1951 by B & I Publishing Co.

Black Cat Mystery was one of the most successful of Harvey Publications's line of pretty rough horror comics in the early '50s.

©1951 by Harvey Features Syndicate

company's long-lived series of one-shots, it offered six stories, fairly adult in attitude though tame in the overt depiction of blood and gore. The leadoff story dealt with a man haunted by the ghost of a stuffed tiger, another with a shipwreck on an island of man-eating lizards, a third with a fellow who thinks he's murdered his wife by shoving her in the path of a subway train and then is hounded by her bloody corpse. The names of the issue's scriptwriters are lost to history, but the artists included Fred Kida, George Roussos, and Joe Kubert.

Eerie, after establishing the horror genre, went into a cataleptic state and didn't return until 1951, when it showed up as a regularly published comic. In the interim, the American Comics Group had come along with *Adventures Into the Unknown*, which was introduced in the fall of 1948. A fairly restrained title, it offered a wide range of horror material each issue— witchcraft, ghosts, monsters, even an adaptation of Horace Walpole's 18th century Gothic novel *The Castle of Otranto. Adventures Into the Unknown* was the first regularly issued horror

comic book and it remained in business for nearly twenty years.

The Marvel/Atlas folks, sensing a trend, began to convert to horror in 1949. *Marvel Mystery* became *Marvel Tales* and for two issues (#74 and #75) *Captain America* was known as *Captain America's Weird Tales*. Many of Marvel's superhero titles had been rich in horrors, especially during the World War II years, when costumed crimebusters were menaced not only by stretch racks and boiling lead, but by zombies, vampires, and werewolves who labored in the employ of the Nazis and Japanese.

Harvey was primarily known for harmless kid titles like *Casper* and *Little Dot*, contrasting sharply with its horror titles.

©1953 by Harvey Features Syndicate

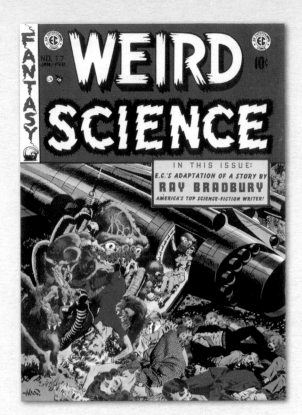

EC Comics publisher William Gaines always claimed to be proudest of his science fiction titles. *Weird Science* #17 features striking cover art by industry legend Wally Wood.

©1952 by Fables Publishing Co., Inc.

"Ghastly" Graham Ingels drew this atmospheric cover to illustrate his story "Poetic Justice." The genuinely eerie illustration is typical of Ingels's spidery style.

©1952 by Fables Publishing co., Inc.

What Marvel did now was keep the horror elements and dump most of the heroes. Harvey followed suit in 1951 by discarding its longtime crimefighter the Black Cat, and converting her magazine to *Black Cat Mystery*.

Young William Gaines was another comic book publisher who noted the new interest in horror. He had inherited the Educational Comics company from his father, M.C. Gaines, in 1947. Among the EC magazines then being published were *Tiny Tot Comics* and the various *Picture Stories* titles. The younger Gaines

favored a more blatantly commercial emphasis. He changed the meaning of the EC acronym to Entertaining Comics and added such tides as *Crime Patrol*, *Gunfighter*, *Modern Love*, and *Saddle Justice*. In 1948 Gaines hired artist-writer Al Feldstein, a graduate of the Iger shop. Feldstein soon became an editor and in 1950 the EC horror line was born.

Gaines has recalled, "Feldstein and I were working along, putting out this crap, and suddenly talking—because we talked a lot, of course—realized that we

both had similar interests in suspense and horror stuff. I grew up on horror pulps and *The Witch's Tale* on the radio and things like that, and at that point they had things on television like *Suspense*, *Lights Out*, *Inner Sanctum*, so we just started doing that kind of story in our crime books." Real horror comics soon followed for EC.

EC's *Weird Fantasy*, *Weird Science*, *The Haunt of Fear*, *Tales From the Crypt*, and *The Vault of Horror* were all born in 1950. The last three featured sardonically funny, and ugly, hosts ▶

The EC Artists

Unsold EC horror comics were stripped of their covers, stapled together beneath a new cover in bunches of four, and sold as annuals. Fans loved them. This spooky-yet-funny 1952 cover was drawn by the multitalented Al Feldstein.

©1952 by Educational Comics, Inc.

While many fans admire EC Comic's well-crafted scripts, it is the exceptional artwork that piques the interest and admiration of collectors. Publisher William Gaines and his editors, Al Feldstein and Harvey Kurtzman, gathered together an impressive crew.

One of the earliest recruits was Johnny Craig, who signed on in the late 1940s after a stint as assistant to artist Sheldon Mayer. Craig started out on *War Against Crime* and Bill Gaines's other early magazines, and later contributed to such titles as *The Vault of Horror* and *The Haunt of Fear*. He drew in a sophisticated, crisply illustrative style that showed the influence of Milton Caniff as well as of the slick magazine illustrators of the period. Craig drew a great many of the EC covers, including the infamous severed head image that graced the cover of *Crime SuspenStories* #22 (May 1954).

The enormously talented Wally Wood went to work for EC in the late 1940s, initially in tandem with artist (and later science-fiction novelist) Harry Harrison. Wood had worked for numerous publishers, but once said he knew he'd "found a home" at EC. Although not an outstanding draftsman, Wood was a master storyteller whose affinities for action and the dramatic interplay of light and shadow were unparalleled. The science-fiction stories he drew for EC's *Weird Science* and *Weird Fantasy* are particularly impressive, and are filled with elegantly rendered rocketships, gruesomely tentacled monsters, and—most memorably—the curvy, full-lipped "Wood women" that became one of his trademarks. He was an able parodist, as well, as he demonstrated in the pages of *Mad*. There, he aped the styles of Walt Kelly, the Disney artists, and many others, to hilarious effect. A true giant of comic book history, Wood made important contributions to the superhero revival of the 1960s and '70s, and remained active until failing eyesight curtailed his output in the late 1970s. He died in 1981.

Jack Davis is the most prolific graduate of EC. An eccentric cartoonist with a flair for caricature, he came to EC in the early 1950s, after having worked as an inker on *The Saint* newspaper strip. His bold, exaggerated style was equally suited to EC's horror, war, and humor comics. "I'm a cartoonist, not an illustrator," he has always insisted. Since the early 1960s Davis has had a very successful career in commercial art, drawing movie posters, cartoons for print advertisements, and covers for such magazines as *Time and TV Guide*.

The greatest of EC's horror artists was Graham Ingels, a quiet, reserved man who had logged many years for other comic book publishers before coming to EC in the late forties. He'd drawn everything from cowboys to spacemen in that decade, but found his niche in the EC horror titles. His spidery renderings of decaying mansions, wizened old crones, and scheming husbands and wives are the stuff of nightmare. If comic books have produced a talent equal to Bosch, it is Graham Ingels.

Among the many other artists who enhanced their reputations by working for EC were science-fiction specialist Al Williamson, manic humorist Will Elder, "good girl" artist Jack Kamen, horror and aviation specialist George Evans, the brilliant draftsman Reed Crandall, and onetime Wally Wood assistant Joe Orlando. In addition, the company occasionally used Russ Heath, Alex Toth, Frank Frazetta, Gene Colan, and Joe Kubert.

THE PUTRID ODOR OF THIRTY-TWO DECAYING CORPSES BURNED THE TRAPPED COUNCILMEN'S NOSTRILS...

OH, LORD! HELP US!

WE'RE TRAPPED! AND THEY'RE COMING...

EEEEEAAAA!

Jack Davis illustrated "Graft in Concrete," a tale in *The Vault of Horror* #26 that concerns murderous councilmen who get their just desserts.

©1952 by L. L. Publishing Co., Inc.

EC was well ahead in horror-comics quality, but Marvel—as Atlas—was first in sheer quantity. *Strange Tales* (right) and *Astonishing* (below) were just two of omre than a dozen horror titles published under the Atlas imprint.

©1952 by Comic Combine   ©1952, 1954 by 20th Century Comics

—The Old Witch, the Crypt Keeper, and the Vault Keeper, respectively—who introduced each issue's quartet of tales, and who showed up again at the conclusion of each to make an appropriately ironic comment. Feldstein did most of the early scripting (he had help later from Carl Wessler, Jack Oleck, and others) and the artwork was provided by the likes of Jack Kamen, Johnny Craig, Graham Ingels (who signed his horror stories "Ghastly"), Wallace Wood, Quality Comics veteran Reed Crandall, Jack Davis, Bernard Krigstein, and Harvey Kurtzman. Actually, Kurtzman limited his early EC work to the science-fiction titles, refusing to work on the horror books. He's said, "The business of playing with dead bodies—stories about chopping people into baseball fields and making their intestines into Christmas ribbons. That's not the kind of thing that I liked to subject my child to."

Kurtzman's reservations aside, Al Feldstein quickly settled into a groove of writing a story a day. He and Gaines had a facile way with the O. Henry style of twist endings, and a love of poetic justice—usually taken to absurd extremes. The archetypal EC horror story was, in fact, called "Poetic Justice" (*Haunt of Fear* #12, April 1952). In it, a kindly junkman is driven to suicide after being sent cruel, anonymous Valentines by a rich man and his sneering son. The junkman is buried, but rises from his grave one year later to avenge his own death. In the story's last panel, the rich man unwraps a Valentine package containing the sticky heart of his son.

Feldstein's variations on this sort of story were ingenious, and although many of the EC horror stories were well written (a few were even adapted from the works of Ray Bradbury) and handsomely illustrated, they did tend to cross boundaries hitherto uncrossed in comic books. As EC historian E. B. Boatner has pointed out, "EC horror opened new vistas of death from sources previously unimagined by the reader. Victims were serial-sectioned by giant machines, eaten by ghouls, devoured by rats—from inside and out—pecked by pigeons, stuffed down disposals, skewered on swords, buried alive, dismembered and used as baseball equipment, hung as living clappers in huge bells, made into sausage and soap, dissolved, southern-fried, hacked up by maniacs in Santa Claus suits, and offed in unusually high percentages by their wives or husbands."

EC had pioneered a new kind of horror comic based not in myth and fantasy but in the banal horrors that, just maybe, could be taking place behind the closed doors of any business or suburban home. These powerfully illustrated melodramas especially appealed to adolescents and young adults who may not have read other, milder comics. Feldstein's scripts were wordy and caption-heavy— more like short stories than comic book tales. Even at their best, though, EC's horror stories were models of blunt simplicity. The value system apparent in Feldstein's scripts was one that had no shadings of gray, no ambiguity. Good people were totally good and evil people were irredeemably, consistently evil. Innocents often suffered, but the guilty suffered

The quality of Harvey's *Witches Tales* varied, but readers could always count on plenty of lurid fun.

©1952, 1953 by Witches Tales, Inc.

DC's *House of Mystery* was vaguely suspenseful but not scary enough to give the average child any nightmares.

©1951, 1952 by DC Comics, Inc.

even more. To unsophisticated readers —particularly adolescents who felt buffeted by teachers, bullies, and other forces beyond their control—this sort of ham-fisted morality was like manna.

After sales figures had established that the EC horror formula was a success, fright comics came creeping onto the stands from a horde of publishers, making the early 1950s the heyday of horror. *Weird Adventures*, *Weird Horrors*, *Weird Thrillers*, *Weird Terror*, *Weird Mysteries*, and *Weird Tales of the Future* could be found crouching beside *Web of Evil*, *Web of Mystery*, *Tomb of Terror*, *Horrific*, *Fantastic Fears*, *Journey into Fear*, *Strange Tales*, *The Horrors*, *Witches' Tales*, and *Uncanny Tales*. Additional horror titles numbered in the dozens.

A great many of the stories recounted in this swarm of magazines were dreadful, and frightening only in their lack of merit and restraint. The more unimaginative publishers took only the roughest, most obvious elements of the EC formula and mated them with wretched scripting and crude, ugly drawing. "Horror comics began to show more gore, more violence, ever more explicitly," science fiction writer and horror comics authority Lawrence Watt-Evans has observed. "It became a matter of topping what had come before; if one issue showed a man killing his wife, the next would top *that*

Mummies, demons, the living dead, and sudden death were among the most familiar themes of horror comics of the early 1950s. Parents didn't appreciate all the gore, but kids ate it up.

©1952 by Animirth Comics, Inc.; ©1951 by DC Comics, Inc.; ©1954 by 20th Century Comics; ©1953 by Prime Publications, Inc.

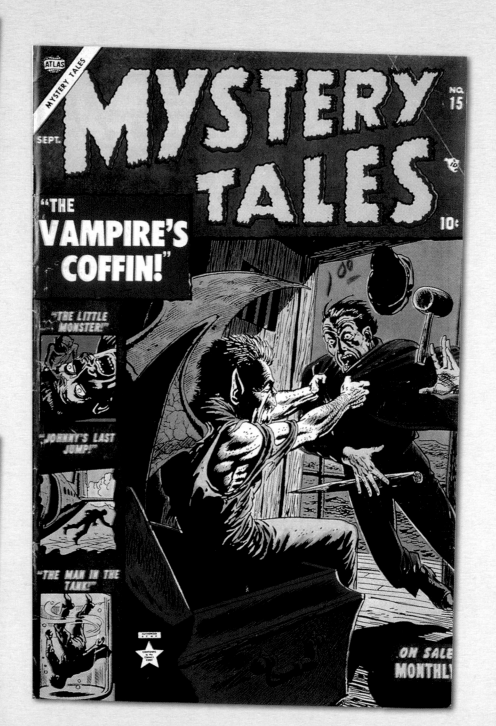

Vampires and phantoms were popular, too, but not nearly as salesworthy as underdressed young women. Artist L. B. Cole's colorful cover for *Terrifying Tales* #15 (bottom left) is a prime example.

by having him hack his wife to pieces, and the next would top that by having him eat her corpse!"

Parents had not paid much attention to Junior's reading habits when he was absorbed in *Superman* and *Jingle Jangle*. But when rough horror comics began showing up under Junior's bed, parents took a second look. Educators, too, began to grow concerned. Transparent, halfhearted attempts from within the comics industry to regulate its own product in the very early 1950s had come to naught. Like some cow town in the Old West, comic books were wide open.

A portent of bad times to come was sounded in 1953, when EC stepped over the line it had itself defined, running a story called "Foul Play" in *Haunt of Fear* #19 (June 1953). In it, an unscrupulous baseball star takes out an opposing player by sliding into the man while wearing poisoned spikes. The victim dies and his teammates discover who's responsible. The story's final panels show a peculiar baseball game, played at midnight beneath the light of the moon. The only players are the teammates of the murdered man. The killer is there, too: His intestines mark the baselines and his legs are the bats. His torso is worn by the catcher as a chest protector. The murderer's scalp is used to brush off home plate, and his head—one eye hanging from its socket—is the ball. This lapse into bad taste shocked even the artist, Jack Davis.

The excesses of "Foul Play" and the decapitations, stabbings, burnings with acid, and sparsely clad young women who were the victims in most of the industry's horror comics didn't go unnoticed by unsympathetic eyes. Ironically, it was the readers of horror novels and viewers of monster movies who probably knew better than anyone else what might befall the publishers of horror comics. Much like the fictional mad scientists who create uncontrollable monsters, the horror publishers had tampered with forbidden things—a transgression that always leads to retribution. Bela Lugosi and Boris Karloff always got their comeuppance, and so would the comic book industry.

In the meantime, sales figures were high and the comic book business was booming. Joe Simon and Jack Kirby, who never completely turned their backs on heroes, tried to buck the trend toward violence in 1946, when they produced two issues of *Stuntman* for Harvey. Their red-clad hero specialized in crimes that centered around Hollywood. This was bravura, slam-bang material, with two-page splash panels that outdid anything the pair had offered in *Captain America*. Sadly, *Stuntman* folded after just three issues.

Simon and Kirby also produced two issues of *The Boy Explorers* in 1946, but only the first issue received proper distribution. The pair's hero product was as inherently appealing as before, but the times were no longer sympathetic to this sort of thing. S & K's *Boy's Ranch*, combining the kid gang idea with the western, followed in 1950 and lasted less than a year.

As superheroes declined, categories that had previously been neglected were expanded. The Korean War began in the summer of 1950 and this inspired a flood of combat comic books. Before the conflict came to a negotiated end in 1953, several dozen war comics, by no means devoted exclusively to the fighting in Korea, had come into being. Where there had earlier been just a handful—such as Dell's *War Comics* and *War Heroes* and Famous Funnies's *Heroic* in the 1940s—there were now many. Marvel publisher Martin Goodman's war effort was especially impressive. Among the more than two dozen war titles he published in the early 1950s, usually under the Atlas colophon, were Battle Action, Battlefield, Battle Brady, Marines In Action, Navy Tales, and Young Men on the Battlefield. DC offered Our Fighting Forces, Our Army At War, Star Spangled War Stories, and All-American Men of War.

EC, with Harvey Kurtzman editing, was responsible for the industry's most politically liberal and literate war titles, *Frontline Combat* and *Two-Fisted Tales*. These were carefully researched and believably drawn by such top-notch talents as John Severin, Reed Crandall, George Evans, and Kurtzman himself. The EC war titles and many of those from other publishers eventually faded from the scene, but the genre had been so firmly established that many of the combat books remained successful sellers until the Vietnam War.

Comic book supermen were also besieged by cowboys. DC turned *All Star* and *All-American* (later to be a war book) into western titles and added *Western Comics*, *Jimmy Wakley*, and *Dale*

This exceptional cover by Simon & Kirby for *Stuntman* #2 sums up the kinetic appeal of the team's flamboyant postwar superhero.

©1946 by Harvey Features Syndicate

One of the only bright spots of the American experience in Korea was the impressive combat performance of U.S. jet fighters. Superior's *Fighting Air Force* celebrated the excitement.

©1952 by Superior Publishers Limited

The Korean War created an audience for war comics. Marvel's *Man Comics*, previously a potpourri of crime and adventure stories, became a war title with issue #9.

©1951 by Newsstand Publications, Inc.

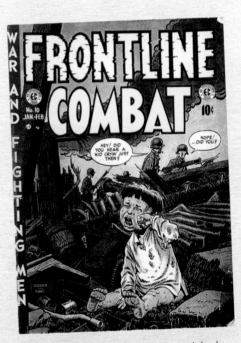

The best (and most humanizing) war comic books were *Two-Fisted Tales* and *Frontline Combat*, both published by EC. This dramatic cover was penciled by John Severin and inked by Bill Elder.

©1952 by Tiny Tot Publications

Fueled by the growth of television, western comics flourished throughout the 1950s. Some, such as *Roy Rogers* and *Gene Autry*, featured movie and TV cowboy stars. Others, like *Ghost Rider*, offered characters unique to comics.

©1951 by Magazine Enterprises, Inc.; ©1951 by Gene Autry;
©1948 by The Lone Ranger, Inc.; ©1952 by Roy Rogers Enterprises

Evans. No piker, Marvel gave the public over fifty different cowboy comics. These included *Kid Colt*, *The Ringo Kid*, *The Texas Kid*, *The Rawhide Kid*, *The Outlaw Kid*, *The Two-Gun Kid*, *The Arizona Kid*, *The Apache Kid* and *The Kid From Texas*. Kid stuff, to be sure, but plenty profitable. Fawcett and Dell emphasized movie cowboys such as Roy Rogers, Bill Boyd, Gene Autry, Gabby Hayes, Tom Mix, Ken Maynard, Monte Hale, Rocky Lane, and Lash LaRue. By the time Victor Fox got around to licensing a cowboy, he had to settle for Hoot Gibson.

Satirical humor became another salable commodity in the early 1950s. EC blazed the way in the autumn of 1952 when it introduced *Mad*. Edited by Kurtzman, this was a comic book version of the college humor magazine of the day as filtered through the eclectic mind of its editor. Early on, *Mad* specialized in hilarious spoofs of famous characters from newspaper comic strips and comic books. Soon, the focus of the magazine's humor broadened to include TV and movies, politics, and daily life.

"Ever since *Mad* started, I've heard twenty stories about who was responsible for *Mad*'s creation," Harvey Kurtzman once said. "As I remember it, I became desperate to do a quick comic. I wasn't making any money with the war books. . . . So I somehow convinced Gaines that I should do something else that was easier. He said 'Go ahead.' Now, I'd always been doing satire in school, in the streets; it was my kind of clowning. . . . The format would make fun of comic books as they were at that particular period."

EC publisher William Gaines has concurred with Kurtzman's recollection of the comic's genesis. "Our official reason for publishing *Mad* was, we were tired of the horror, weary of the science fiction, ▶

Harvey Kurtzman

Among the several awards given out by fans each year for achievement in the comic book field are the Harvey Awards. These are named in honor of Harvey Kurtzman, and place him in the comic book pantheon with Will Eisner and Jack Kirby, who also enjoy the distinction of having had annual awards named after them. While not as prolific or as committed to the medium as other important artists, Kurtzman has been tremendously influential.

He was born in New York in 1924 and began to draw professionally for comic books while still a teenager. Most of Kurtzman's early work was in the superhero genre. In the middle 1940s, after leaving the service, he established a commercial art studio. By this time his style had changed and his *Hey Look!* humor filler pages, which graced various Marvel titles, were done with the loose, bold brushwork that became his trademark.

Kurtzman went to work for William Gaines at EC in 1950. He did horror and suspense stories for a time, then created and edited EC's *Two-Fisted Tales* and *Frontline Combat*. "All our stories protested war," he has been quick to assert.

A very thorough writer-editor, Kurtzman usually provided page layouts for his artists, and encouraged them to do historical research in order to be as accurate as possible. The EC war stories were set not just during World War II and the Korean conflict, but during ancient Rome, the Crusades, the American Revolution, the Napoleonic era, the Civil War, World War I, and many other fascinating periods. These war stories, many of them drawn by Kurtzman himself, are the finest ever seen in comic books.

Following the success of the EC war titles, Kurtzman created *Mad*. A ten-cent, full-color comic book for its first twenty-three issues, it sold briskly and went on to become a cultural icon that inspired innumerable comic book and magazine-format imitations.

Kurtzman left EC shortly after *Mad* converted to magazine format in 1955. He went on to edit and contribute to a trio of short-lived but worthy humor magazines—*Trump*, *Humbug*, and *Help!* He also created the saucy, long-running *Little Annie Fanny* strip for *Playboy*, bringing with him onetime *Mad* artist Will Elder. Kurtzman passed away in 1993, leaving behind him a body of work that remains highly popular and influential.

The 1950s brought a quartet of new American magazines that became enormously successful: *Sports Illustrated*, *TV Guide*, *Playboy*, and . . . *Mad Magazine*. The first cover features a parody of the horror comics EC was known for.

©1952 by Educational Comics, Inc.

we wanted to do a *comic* comic. That was not true; it was just publicity. It was so Kurtzman could get a fifty percent raise."

As Gaines remembered it, "*Mad* lost money for three issues. 'Superduperman' [Kurtzman's parody of Superman, drawn by Wally Wood] was in issue #4. *Mad* then became popular." So popular that other publishers quickly stepped in with imitations. "Martin Goodman had half a dozen," Gaines once said. "There were seventy titles, I understand; my printer counted them up because he used to keep a list of all comics published. And he told me there were seventy. I think he was wrong, but there were certainly thirty, forty or fifty imitations of *Mad*. You know, *Eek, Ecch, Oook* . . . I can't remember them all."

Well, there was no *Oook*, but included among the earliest actual imitations of *Mad* were EC's own *Panic* (edited by Al Feldstein) and many (shortlived) titles from other publishers—*Crazy, Riot, Eh!, Madhouse, Get Lost, Whack,* and *Nuts!* Most of the knockoffs aped *Mad*'s irreverence, but none came close to its sophistication and innate cleverness. Even EC's *Panic* seems labored.

Although not every comic book of the period was an artistic success, sales figures proved that the industry had met the postwar challenge, coming up with several successful alternatives to the declining superhero genre. Horror, war,

jungle girls, cowboys, romance, humor —they all sold briskly. Millions of dollars were still being made as publishers responded to shifting demographics by producing humor, romance, and horror books to suit.

Bill Elder's "Frank N. Stein" appeared in *Mad* #8 in 1953. Manic yet devoted to detail, Elder later worked with Harvey Kurtzman on *Little Annie Fanny*, a popular and long-running feature of *Playboy* magazine.

©1953 by Educational Comics, Inc.

TALES CALCULATED TO DRIVE YOU

MAD

No. 9 MARCH

10¢

HUMOR IN A JUGULAR VEIN

THE BAD ONES ARE COMING, MARSHAL.....BUT AS LONG AS I HOLD YOU, I AM NOT AFRAID, FOR I KNOW YOU ARE NOT AFRAID!

H. Kurtz-

Harvey Kurtzman's wit and infallible sense of design elevate this early *Mad* cover that spoofs the film *High Noon*.

©1953 by Educational Comics, Inc.